W9-BRD-916

THE

7 PRINCIPLES OF PUBLIC SPEAKING

GCLS/GLASSBORO BRANCH
2 CENTER STREET
GLASSBORO, NJ 08028

THE

7PRINCIPLES OF PUBLIC SPEAKING

PROVEN METHODS FROM A PR PROFESSIONAL

RICHARD ZEOLI

Skyhorse Publishing, Inc.

Copyright © 2008 by Richard Zeoli

All Rights Reserved. No part of this book may be reproduced in
any manner without the express written consent of the publisher,
except in the case of brief excerpts in critical reviews or articles. All
inquiries should be addressed to Skyhorse Publishing, 555 Eighth
Avenue, Suite 903, New York, NY 10018.

Skyhorse Publishing books may be purchased in bulk at special
discounts for sales promotion, corporate gifts, fund-raising, or
educational purposes. Special editions can also be created to
specifications. For details, contact the Special Sales Department,
Skyhorse Publishing, 555 Eighth Avenue, Suite 903, New York, NY
10018 or info@skyhorsepublishing.com.

www.skyhorsepublishing.com

10 9 8 7 6 5 4 3 2 1

Library of Congress Cataloging-in-Publication Data

Zeoli, Richard.
The seven principles of public speaking : proven methods from a
PR professional / Richard Zeoli.
p. cm.
Includes bibliographical references and index.
ISBN 978-1-60239-283-0 (alk. paper)
1. Public speaking. I. Title.
PN4129.15.Z46 2008
808.5'1--dc22
2008031481

Printed in China

This book is dedicated to all the brave souls who understand that the credit in life truly does belong to those who are in the arena

and

to Brigid, my best friend and the love of my life.

Special thanks to the following people for their help in this process:
Anthony Skalicky, Jr., for creating the "Speaker's Message" graphic
Gina Diorio for her attention to detail
Debbi Bifulco, for keeping me on task, and
Bill Wolfsthal and everyone at Skyhorse Publishing for transforming this vision into reality.

Contents

THE POWER OF COMMUNICATION

Improve Your Life...

Grow Your Business...

Change the World

The Power of Communication

What This Book Can Do For You

This book can greatly help you to improve your communication skills, and this will have a direct impact on your mental, emotional, vocational, and financial destiny.

Imagine having greater confidence in every situation in which you are required to state your case, persuade someone important, articulate your feelings, sell your product, negotiate, ask for a raise, or interview for your dream job.

The fact is that these principles can and should be used every time you communicate, whether it is in a public setting or not. The skills that will ensure you are a more confident communicator in a roomful of people are the same skills you should apply when speaking one-on-one with another person.

Unquestionably, there are challenges in life. I firmly believe every challenge is an opportunity for us to think more creatively, hone our skills, and improve our destiny. Once we embrace challenge as a necessary part of life, we realize our potential to overcome challenges and reach greater success.

And I truly believe that, with few exceptions, human beings overcome their challenges through communication.

Think about it.

When we are challenged in our personal lives with our spouse or our children, we often achieve harmony through communication, through talking about the problem in depth and finding solutions based on love. Sometimes the problem stems from the fact that we haven't communicated our love in the first place.

When we are challenged at work or we feel as if we are not truly being recognized for our talents and our efforts, it is often because we have not properly communicated those efforts in the first place. Many people are surprised to find that the reason they haven't earned a raise or a promotion is that they haven't communicated their desire to get one. Even more people are surprised to realize that very often the reason their efforts in the office go unnoticed is that if they have communicated their efforts, they have not done so to the right people.

Even some of the gravest problems the world faces can be solved through effective communication and, many times, the problems are a direct result of the fact that two or more parties—or nations—have not been communicating in the first place.

Regardless of your level of experience, you can immediately improve your personal or occupational situation and become a more confident communicator by applying the seven principles found in this book. How many high level CEOs would love to retract statements they made when they weren't adequately prepared for a crisis or when they were trying to project an image and their words back fired?

Conversely, isn't it wonderful when we watch effective communicators in action? This applies to not only the famous speeches of communication giants like Dr. Martin Luther King, Margaret Thatcher, and Gandhi, but also the great oratorical achievements of ordinary people from all walks of life who stand up to communicate with pride and determination.

Our greatest asset in the world is communication. Written and verbal communication has freed slaves, conquered nations, ended oppression, created great wealth, changed lives, destroyed lives, created peace, started wars, and led to both success and failure. Communication can be used for good and for bad, and this is why it is critical that we always use this power for good. As you master the principles in this book, you will discover an increased ability to persuade people to a certain way of thinking. But with this ability comes responsibility to ensure that the way of thinking in question is correct and not harmful.

People crave leadership, and skilled communicators have an incredible ability to bring that leadership into people's lives—to bring hope and light into even the darkest places. Effective communicators also have the ability to reassure people during times of crisis and to motivate people toward greatness. True greatness.

- If you are a manager, this book will give you the skills to confidently speak to your team and motivate them to greater heights.

- If you are an entrepreneur, this book will give you the skills to confidently present your dream to the rest of the world and grow your business.
- If you are a leader in any industry or venture, this book will help you convey your message and persuade others to follow your vision.

You have within you the tools necessary to achieve greatness and bring increased prosperity, joy, peace, and love into your life and into the lives of those around you. Yes, effective communication can and will help you achieve success, and these seven principles will be the key that unlocks the great potential inside you.

Good luck, and enjoy the journey.

A NEW PARADIGM

THE PUBLIC SPEAKING JOURNEY

Timeless Principles versus

Techniques and Gimmicks

A NEW PARADIGM

You walk into your company boardroom. Seated all around the table are the most important people in your professional life—all with eyes fixed on you. These people can make or break your career and you have to speak in front of them. Yet, for the first time in your life, you feel a sense of confidence and calm you've never felt before. As you walk to the front of that boardroom, you look each and every person in the eye. You feel relaxed. You feel confident. You feel ready to make a connection with this audience. They are looking at you. They are ready to hear you speak.

You open your mouth and the words come out effortlessly. The words flow. You can see in the eyes of your audience that they are truly listening to you. You are making a human connection with your audience. This is one of the most magical feelings that we can ever experience—to connect with our fellow human beings.

And it feels great.

You deliver your message. It's powerful. It's concise. It's effective. And the people in that room enjoy it. You feel that they are with you. You sense that they are hanging on your words. Time seems fluid. You realize that you are in control of the situation. And when it's over, you get a round of applause. You know that your professional career is set because of the words that came out of your mouth in that crucial moment of your life.

Wouldn't it be great if that scenario could happen to you every day?

The Genesis of the Principles

There were moments in my life when I stood before audiences, and I knew that they were with me. It was an incredible feeling, a magical feeling, really, when time seemed to slow down and the words I spoke seemed to come out so effortlessly and so gracefully. I felt like a star athlete in the zone, totally incapable of anything other than success, as if all of my operations were on autopilot. When the speech was over, I didn't even remember what I had said; it was as if my conscious brain weren't even around.

I was in the zone.

But there were other times I flat-out stunk.

I was long-winded and verbose. The crowd was bored—it's not just that they weren't with me for *part* of the speech—they were *never* with me. From the minute I started talking, I wasn't able to connect with them. During those times, I felt like the kicker on the football team who missed the field goal that would have propelled the team to victory.

Why the disparity?

Many people look at public speaking as something they fear. Others view it as a necessity in their daily lives. I view public speaking as an art, a fundamental communication tool that really enables the speaker to be more than him or her self. When we communicate with an audience, connect with our fellow human beings, it is a very special feeling. To be able to overcome our fears, look our peers in their eyes, and speak before them is something very important—and not necessarily something that may come easily.

In this day and age, communication is one of the most important and crucial ingredients to success. People who are able to communicate well have an advantage that stands out from the rest. We all know people who are well educated and well qualified, but were passed over in life for someone more eloquent. Effective communication truly levels the playing field, and this is great news for many of us. I wasn't born wealthy, and I certainly wasn't the best student in my class. My dad is a retired police officer, and he raised our family with modest means and prepared me for the world. But soon after college, when I entered the workplace, I realized how people with Ivy League credentials or family pedigree had a distinct advantage: They were able to get in the door of places I could only dream of. But I learned early on that I had a gift as a speaker, and I could connect with an audience.

I made a commitment to myself to develop that skill and soon learned that it provided me with unforeseen advantages. There are incredibly smart people who simply cannot communicate well. Most companies whose lifeblood depends on sales—and let's face it, what company's lifeblood doesn't?—would choose a gifted communicator over a person who earned straight As but can't get on his feet and confidently connect with other people.

This opportunity—this gift, this advantage—can be yours.

When my publisher first approached me about writing this book, the question he had was, "What makes this book different?" To answer that question, I need to tell you a story. (By the way, you will find that the power of storytelling is your greatest tool as a speaker, and it should be used frequently to connect with people.)

Early in my career as a speaker, I was asked to give a motivational speech at a leadership training program in New Jersey. I would be speaking to several hundred young leaders about making a difference in the world. My speech was rewarded with tremendous applause, and soon I was approached by the management and asked if I would develop a public speaking course for the program's participants. In writing the course, I focused on technique, which is emphasized by many public speaking books and courses: how to use good eye contact, how to project, how to use proper body language. The course focused on how to write a basic speech, how to use note cards, and how to tell a joke. But something was missing. The participants were certainly benefiting from the class—after all, they were learning valuable skills—but I could see in their eyes that there was something deeper about human communication that I was missing. Something that I had yet to find in a book or a course. Something only life and experience would reveal to me in time.

But then was not the time.

Years passed, and I found myself on national television facing the unsympathetic glare of the camera as millions sat on the other side watching me. I was terrified, and yet in the moment of that great anxiety, I learned a powerful lesson that would soon become the basis of this entire training program. Only I didn't realize the lesson yet. I would first have to make a lot more mistakes along the way.

I wanted to understand how people connected with one another. I wanted to understand how truly great communicators are able to hold an audience in the palm of their hand and convey messages that would change the world. I began to see public speaking as one of the most powerful skills human beings could possess. It gave them the ability to help others and to help themselves.

I wanted to understand it. I wanted to learn. I wanted to be able to put my finger on why certain speakers were great and why others simply weren't. I had read books on communication, and they were very helpful in explaining the science of communication, and many even offered useful techniques on how to be a good speaker, how to prepare a winning presentation, and how to make the audience laugh.

But something was still missing.

I knew how to give a good speech most of the time. I knew how to create a presentation that would get my message across in a persuasive and informative way. But I still didn't understand why I could really connect with an audience on some days but not others. The human connection with an audience is one of the most magical feelings you can ever experience, and I wanted to achieve it every time I spoke, not just once in a while.

Imagine if every time you had to make a presentation in front of your company, or sell your business, or persuade an audience, you were able to knock the ball out of the park. Not just once in a while, but each and every time. As I began to pay attention to my own experiences as a speaker, I began to understand that the use of certain core fundamentals virtually guaranteed that I would be successful every time I stood up to speak. In fact, when I didn't rely on those core fundamentals, that aching, nagging feeling returned, and I realized that I was not connecting with my audience.

I focused on developing those fundamentals, and I wrote them down. They became the foundation for the book you are now holding in your hands—*The 7 Principles of Public Speaking*. After studying the masters, spending time with accomplished speakers, and learning through years of trial and error, I soon realized that there are principles that must be mastered if you want to be a truly effective communicator.

That is what makes this book different.

It is not about technique. It is about timeless principles which, when applied, will help you achieve the success you have always imagined. If you are a beginner, these principles will help you overcome your anxiety, conquer your fear, and achieve results. If you are an experienced speaker, these principles will take you to the next level of effectiveness.

Most public speaking books that focus on techniques fall short of making a lasting impact for one very important reason: they neglect to recognize that public speaking is a journey. Watch a young JFK giving a speech as a congressman and then compare that to his 1960 inaugural address. Listen to Barack Obama stumble in the early presidential debates or

Ronald Reagan try to wow a crowd long before he became "the Great Communicator." You'll recognize quickly that communicators grow and transform over time.

Most people, however—because they view speaking as a "once in a while/only if I have to" occurrence—do not grow. They remain stagnant as communicators, not recognizing the potential emotional, spiritual, and vocational growth that awaits those who embark on a journey toward becoming truly effective communicators.

After spending the majority of my life speaking, training, and coaching, I believe it is time for a public speaking paradigm shift. It is time for colleges and universities to completely throw away their previous methods of teaching public speaking (which do little more than explain how to write a speech and use good eye contact), and start teaching public speaking as an exciting journey. It is time for individuals to stop viewing public speaking as something that happens as infrequently as a holiday, and recognize the opportunity that exists all around for communication to drastically improve their lives, grow their businesses, help them land better jobs, enhance their relationships, increase their self-esteem, and develop their potential in ways they never before knew existed.

It is time for people to recognize that public speaking is not some hidden mystery but in reality, nothing more than communicating, and in this, public speaking is no different from having a conversation.

Yes, it's time to recognize that effective communication can be one of the most fulfilling experiences we as humans will ever enjoy.

It is also time to recognize that public speaking—whether by the best man making a heartfelt toast at a wedding, a speaker who inspires tens of thousands to action, the ignoramus who makes an offensive joke in an attempt to lighten the mood, or the person who eulogizes a loved one and brings comfort to a grieving family—is universal.

Public speaking, when done well, like fine wine or classical music, shows the potential we have as people and brings us that much closer to our true potential. With nothing more than words, we are capable of starting wars, ending wars, causing markets to tumble, and reassuring millions after a national tragedy. That is truly an amazing reality to ponder.

Our Greatest Fear?

Why is it that the thought of public speaking terrifies so many people? Why is it that public speaking is consistently listed among our biggest fears? The great comedian, Jerry Seinfeld, once said, "More people fear public speaking than death. Which means if you are like the majority of people, at a funeral, you would rather be in the casket than giving the eulogy." I believe that the reason so many people are petrified of speaking in public is that they have mentally created and replayed scenario after scenario of mistakes, embarrassment, and failure.

Picture yourself in a restaurant. You're preparing to place your breakfast order. Now, under normal circumstances, this is a stress-free activity, right? Well, now, I want you to visualize the following in your mind: Every person in the restaurant has suddenly stopped what they're doing, turned around in their chairs, and started staring at you as you place your breakfast order. Just knowing that all these people are looking at you, you begin to stumble over your words. You mess up the order and you confuse the waiter. Now, everyone in the restaurant is laughing at you. Now, I'm guessing that in a scenario like this, you'd probably rather starve to death than place another breakfast order, but it's a safe bet that very few people avoid restaurants for fear of ordering.

Are Truly Effective Public Speakers Made, or Are They Born?

We turn on the television and see certain people speaking before major crowds or handling an experienced reporter with finesse, and it looks so effortless. In the fifteen years that I've been training people to become more effective communicators, I have watched for common themes among great speakers. Are great speakers made, or are they just born that way? Are they born with a gift that most of us will just never have, or is there something more to it? I have seen major political candidates up close and personal, watched prominent CEOs interviewed on national television, and known of television personalities who experience anxiety before public speaking. I have learned that even the people we think are naturally accomplished public speakers often undergo significant training. While it is true that some individuals are definitely born with a gift, the overwhelming majority of people are effective speakers because they train themselves to be so. Either they have pursued structured public speaking education or coaching, or they have had the opportunity to stand on their feet and deliver speeches on many occasions and have developed their skills over time.

The fact is that public speaking is a skill set that can be learned, and it is a skill set that will continuously improve as time goes on.

And what do great speakers all have in common?

We've all probably been in situations in which we have marveled at speakers who just seem so natural, so relaxed, and so comfortable. And we've probably thought to ourselves, "Wow. I want to be just like them." And we've also wondered, "Did they receive training or were they just born with this gift?" On the flip side, we've also all experienced those situations in which we've had to endure the most painful speeches, listening to speakers who went on and on, or the speaker who was so bad that even he had to admit he was terrible before even beginning to speak. Now, is there any hope for these people or were they just born that way?

And what does the answer to this question mean for you in your own journey to become an effective communicator? In short, what do you, the reader, want to get out of improved public speaking?

Are you willing to take this journey to become an A-level speaker—a truly stellar communicator? Or are you satisfied to remain where you are? Do you want to be able always to command the room—any room, whether it houses your senior managers or 250 people at a political rally? Or are you comfortable just learning a few tricks of the trade to be simply competent?

That is for you, and you alone, to decide.

But to help you make your choice, I have prepared the following Speaker Self-Assessment. As you go through these brief questions, be honest in your answers. Don't respond with what you *wish* were true, but with what actually is true. And don't worry if your answers aren't what you want them to be right now. After all, this book is here to help you make the changes you want to make to become a successful communicator!

Speaker Self-Assessment

What are my greatest strengths as a speaker?

_____

_____

What are my areas of greatest challenge?

_____

_____

On a scale of 1–10 with 1 being nonexistent and 10 being overwhelming:
I would rate my anxiety before the speech as:

_____

I rate my anxiety during the speech as:

_____

I rate my anxiety after the speech as:

_____

For the following two questions, fill in the blank with the first word or phrase that comes to your mind.

I _____ public speaking.

If I were a more effective communicator, I would:

_____

_____

_____

Who is my favorite speaker and why?

_____

_____

_____

Who are some of the most successful people in business? Have they used public speaking to achieve success?

_____

_____

_____

Think of people you know whose business is struggling. Could being a more effective public speaker help them achieve success? How?

_____

_____

_____

If you read this book and apply all the principles I describe, I assure you that communication success will become a reality for you each and every time you get in front of an audience of any size—be it five people or five thousand. This is because the principles are the same, regardless of the size of the group or the nature of the occasion.

As you go through this book, it is very important to read each chapter and complete all of the exercises. This is a book that will unlock your potential and help you achieve the results you have always imagined. If you are among the 99 percent of the population that is afraid of public speaking, this book will help you overcome your fears once and for all.

If you are an experienced speaker, and you understand that even the world's greatest athletes always continuously improve, then this book will be your guide as you take your abilities to new heights. If you are a team leader, use this book with your team and see increased synergy and results.

PRINCIPLE
PERCEPTION 1

Stop Trying to Be a Great Public Speaker

Always bear in mind that your own resolution to succeed is more important than any one thing.

—Abraham Lincoln

PERCEPTION

A very ambitious executive was determined to master the art of public speaking. His desire to improve was intense, and if you have ever joined a public speaking organization, you probably understand his desire. He was a charismatic guy who was blessed with wit and the ability to crack jokes and be lighthearted among his friends. He was the life of the party. So, when he contacted me for public speaking help, I figured this was going to be an easy task.

When he stood in front of the room and started to speak, however, he suddenly changed into a completely different person. The best analogy I can give is that he turned into a robot and started to use this strange voice. I stopped him and said, "Hang on one second here. What are you doing? Where did *you* go?"

He looked at me suspiciously and said, "What do you mean? I'm giving a speech."

I said to him, "Yes, but you're using this different voice and suddenly your whole personality just went away. Where did it go?"

He paused for a few moments, stared me down, and said to me, "But I'm trying to sound like a great public speaker."

Now, I don't know about you, but I would rather not hear from someone who gets up and tries to sound like a robot. To me, that does not make someone a good public speaker. What does? We'll get to that.

If you believe in your heart that you can, in fact, become a great public speaker, then you have the right frame of mind to begin our training. However, if you're like most people and the very thought of giving a speech causes you a lot of anxiety, I need you first to come to understand what public speaking is and what public speaking isn't.

Before we really delve into this book, let's pause for a brief exercise. Please answer a basic but important question for me: What is public speaking?

What is your definition of public speaking?

_____

_____

_____

This first question might seem simple, but it is an important one, and like all the questions in this book, it is vital to your success that you take the time to answer. Maybe you wrote that public speaking is standing behind a podium giving a speech. Perhaps you wrote that public speaking involves large crowds or important topics, or maybe you wrote that public speaking occurs any time you get on your feet in front of a few people. As I said, none of the answers is wrong. Now, look at your answer, and let me ask you a few more questions.

Do public speakers actually need to be standing to give a speech?

Does there have to be a large crowd?

Do there have to be important topics at hand?

There is no right or wrong answer, but I'd like you to take a moment and write down the first thoughts that come to your mind.

President Franklin Delano Roosevelt spoke about incredibly important topics as he struggled to pull the nation out of the Great Depression, but when he gave his fireside chats, he did it from his wheelchair, and he was only speaking into a microphone. So, the question is, "Was he publicly speaking or not?"

As you will soon discover, so much of public speaking is a mental game, and far beyond skill, conquering your thoughts about public speaking is very much the first step on your journey toward becoming a truly effective communicator. So let's put it in everyday terms. Have you gone out to eat at a restaurant lately with a group of some of your friends? What if I told you that when you ordered your dinner you were, in fact, publicly speaking?

Understanding what public speaking truly is, then, is the key to overcoming your fears and becoming an effective communicator. The Merriam-Webster Dictionary defines public speaking as "the act or process of making speeches in public; the art of effective oral communication with an audience." Well, what did you do when you went out to dinner with some of your friends or made conversation over Thanksgiving dinner? Chances are you laughed, had some great conversation, and had a good time.

You might be surprised to realize this, but at Thanksgiving dinner, you were, in fact, having oral communication with an audience. Sure, the audience consisted of your great-aunt and maybe a few cousins whom you secretly hoped would forget to make the trip, but it was still an audience. I've met some of the most entertaining dinner guests in my life who can make everyone at the table feel relaxed and enjoy the evening, but for whatever reason, when they get onstage in front of the very same people or stand up to give a speech in the company boardroom, they freeze and are overcome with anxiety. What changed? Is it the fact that they stood up, or is it the fact that they suddenly realized they were now "publicly speaking"?

The Fundamental Question

If public speaking is the art of effective oral communication with an audience, isn't that what these individuals at the dinner were doing in the first place? Nowhere does the definition of public speaking say that you have to be standing or that you have to be delivering a speech on topics of sweeping world change. All it says is that you have to have effective oral communication with an audience (and notice there isn't even a size requirement).

Please allow me to give you the official definition of public speaking according to the 7 Principles of Public Speaking: *Public speaking occurs any time you talk to anyone and someone else is present to hear you—intentionally or not.*

This means that when you and your wife were discussing the college fund this morning at the local diner, and a few people were in earshot of your conversation, you were actually engaging in public speaking.

Before we get too deep into this point, however, let's understand what public speaking does *not* have to be. It doesn't have to be marked by fiery rhetoric or passionate pleas for change. It doesn't have to be funny. It doesn't have to be long. It doesn't have to be profound. So, what does it have to be?

You know the answer to this already, because you've had to listen to speeches in your life. The best speakers are the ones who do nothing more than have a conversation with their audience. Isn't that really what made FDR so effective in those fireside chats—his ability to talk to the nation over a radio and reassure millions of people that we would survive the Great Depression? In reality, it was a simple conversation that made a great president connect with people in their living rooms. And when we think of successful speakers whom we've heard in life, is it possible that we really like them because they seemed, well, like someone we'd like to have at our dinner table sharing conversation with us?

Please answer a few more questions for me. Think of a speech that you heard that you particularly enjoyed. It could be a speech anywhere. It could have been in your company boardroom. It could be at an arena. It could have been something you heard on television. It really doesn't matter. The point is, I want you to write down a time when someone got up in front of you and talked and it was memorable to you.

Think about what made it memorable.
Who was the speaker?

What struck you about him or her, and how did you feel during the speech?

How did you feel when it was over?

Focus on the human qualities of that speaker.
What did you like about him or her?

How did you feel when you were listening to the speech?

I'm willing to bet that in this exercise, regardless of the speaker you chose, you wrote down things like: "The speaker was personable." "The speaker was relaxed." "The speaker made me feel relaxed." "The speaker made me think that the speech was not going to go on forever." "The speaker made me feel like I knew this person." "The speaker made me feel comfortable." "The speaker had a point." "The speaker gave a clear message." "The speaker made me understand my stake in the process."

Reactions like that are exactly what we want to evoke from our audience.

The best public speakers are those who seem to genuinely enjoy giving a speech. Because they're relaxed, we're relaxed. Great speakers speak *to* us, not *at* us, and the most effective public speaking is a relaxed and comfortable conversation between a speaker and his or her audience.

Stop for a moment and reread this last statement. Isn't this what you do every single day in regular conversation with your friends, family, and co-workers? You talk comfortably, and you speak *with* them, as opposed to *at* them.

It is important to understand and to truly believe in your heart that to master the art of public speaking, all you have to do is be yourself.

That's right.

Learn to Speak Like Yourself

People want to listen to someone who is interesting, relaxed, and comfortable. So, in order to become an effective public speaker, you must accept that the secret lies in letting go of the "public" part and focusing on the speaking part. Begin by having a conversation. If you can carry on a relaxed conversation with one or two people, you can give a great speech. Get over the word "public" and realize that whether your audience consists of two people or two thousand, whether there is a podium not, whether you're talking about the latest medical breakthrough or what you did today at work, it's not about turning into someone you're not in an effort to try to become a great public speaker. It's all about talking to people and making a connection by being yourself.

Focus on this as you learn the rest of the seven principles, and you will be on your way to becoming a truly effective communicator. Trust me; I've learned this from experience.

Many years ago, my younger brother was becoming an Eagle Scout, the highest honor you can receive in scouting. His honor earned him a large, lavish ceremony, and he asked me if I would speak at the ceremony. I was honored. It was one of the best moments of my life. I wrote a speech, and I was really excited because this was a big day for my brother. The day of the ceremony came, and I got up in front of the room and I gave my speech. I was fiery, and I was passionate about how great it is to serve your country. But I wasn't myself. As I look back on that time, I realize that I let a great opportunity pass because I tried to be someone that I'm not.

Now, ten years later, I realize how simple it could have been to make a change before I got up to that podium. If I just would have realized that to be a great speaker I didn't have to change my voice, change my personality, or change who I was, I would have really connected with the audience that day and made a great impact. I believe that, in life, we learn as much from our failures as we do from our successes—maybe even more—and that's why I'm sharing this deeply personal story with you.

As we begin to build together on the seven principles in this book, I want you to understand that you already have within you everything you need to become a truly effective communicator. Don't try to be anything other than who you are.

From Theory to Practice: Making It Work

How do we truly learn to be ourselves when we are giving a presentation? The first concept to understand is that to be an effective speaker, you have to be prepared. Preparation is key and will ensure that you are ready even if you have to give an impromptu presentation—and there is a very good chance that at some point in your life you will have to get up on your feet and speak "off the cuff." But don't worry. We will deal with that challenge as well.

The Speaker Challenge

Understanding Our Reality at the Podium Or, as I Call It, "You are on the Moon; The Audience is at Mission Control"

When you get up in front of an audience of any size to speak, remember this important principle: the relationship between how you feel when you stand up in front of a group and how that group feels about you as the speaker is truly the equivalent of the relationship between the moon and mission control—with you on the moon and the audience watching you back at mission control.

First, you must understand that time feels different for a speaker at the podium (on the moon) than it does for the audience back at mission control. On the moon, a pause feels like an eternity. But back at mission control, it feels just like what it is: a pause that lasted a few seconds. No big deal. And it forces audience members to pay attention to you if their minds have been drifting off.

On the moon, our temptation is to fill the empty space with lots of words, and a long speech feels like we are telling all the relevant points. But back at mission control, a long speech feels like just that: a long speech.

When you make a mistake on the moon, you feel as if everyone else notices and as if your mistake has severely affected the mission. At mission control, they don't even notice, and the mission is still going full speed ahead.

We get nervous when we are about to do a moonwalk because it is unfamiliar territory to us, but once we get going, we tend to relax and feel more comfortable. Back at mission control, they really can't tell we are nervous, and most of the time, they only know it because we tell them after the mission, "I was so nervous!" In other words, mission control only knows what we let them know.

On the moon, we tend to be very focused on facts and want people to know every little detail. Meanwhile, at mission control, they are dreamers and want to hear the exciting stories you have to tell. After all, they are looking up to you.

On the moon, we tend to feel like we are being judged. After all, it's kind of lonely up there. But at mission control, the audience is actually rooting for us. They want to see us succeed because they know that, in reality, we are representing their success today—and their ability to succeed tomorrow. They will have to walk on the moon one day and want people rooting for them when the time comes. If we can do something, so can they.

The Time/Space Difference on the Moon

We have all been taught the theory of relativity. To paraphrase Albert Einstein, "Put your hand on a hot stove for a minute, and it seems like an hour. Sit with a woman you care about for an hour, and it seems like a minute. *That's* relativity."

This kind of relativity is something we experience as a speaker every time we give a presentation.

The first rule we must accept is that time feels different for us when we are on the moon than it does back at mission control. I often encourage my clients to use periodic dramatic pauses in their talks to pull the audience back into consciousness. But most people react by saying that their pause, which should only last a few seconds, feels like an eternity to them. Too often, people are asked a question, and they feel they have to immediately blurt out an answer as if they were being graded on how quickly they answer as opposed to how thoughtful the answer is. Watch carefully when accomplished communicators are handed a question. You will see them take a few seconds to organize their thoughts before giving a carefully constructed answer.

For most of us, however, the idea of taking a few seconds while we are on stage and all eyes are upon us is terrifying. That is because when we are speaking, we experience time very differently than the audience does. The feeling of having everyone look up at us and wait for our every word causes us to feel this way.

The solution: Change your thinking about how time is perceived as a speaker versus as a member of the audience. A pause to you may feel like an eternity, but to the audience, it feels like a mere pause. Take your time. There is no need to rush through your remarks. If you have to rush to fit in your remarks in an allotted time, it is because you didn't follow Principle 7 and the law of anticipation. But let's not get ahead of ourselves.

Knowing Your Audience

The reason we find it so much easier to be ourselves when we are having a conversation with our friends over dinner than we do when we are having a conversation with an audience during a speech is that we know our friends very well. Therefore, your challenge as a speaker is to know your audience almost as well as you know your friends. And you must do this before you have to give your speech. This may sound monumental, but you will be happy to know it is easier than you think.

Audience Research

In most cases, performing a basic search on the Web will tell you a lot about an organization. This is a great tool to use if you are unfamiliar with a group. You should always view the

company's Web site, ask the company to send you its marketing materials, and read the bios of key company personnel.
Knowledge is power, and knowing everything you can about
an organization will help make your time on the moon that
much more comfortable. Plus, the folks at mission control
will truly appreciate that you have taken the time to learn
about them and relate to them during your speech.

There really is no reason that anyone should ever walk into
a presentation without fully understanding his or her audience; yet, I am constantly surprised by the number of people
who do just this. They walk into a room cold. They may have
spent hours writing a great speech; they may have practiced
that speech; they may have even attended training on how to
properly deliver that speech, but they didn't take the time to
do the necessary research to know their audience.

We all appreciate it when someone takes the time to truly
understand our unique needs, wants, and desires. The best salespeople do this on a regular basis, and by doing so, they make
their customers feel like friends and family. These sales pro-
fessionals take the time to know birthdays, anniversaries, and
career milestones. The best salespeople send thank-you notes,
follow-up notes, and even no-reason-in-particular notes.

The best speakers do the same with their audience.

This doesn't mean that you should send everyone in your
audience a personal note, though this is a wonderful idea and
I highly recommend it. What it does mean, however, is that
you should take the time to know as much as possible about
your audience before you ever walk into the room.

Audiences are not usually made up of a random assemblage
of people. In most cases, the audience members have a tre-

mendous amount in common with each other. People tend to associate with like-minded people. That is true in social as well as in business settings. And this gives you as a speaker a tremendous advantage because you can custom-tailor your message for your audience.

Audience analysis checklist:

Where do the majority of the audience members live?

_____

_____

Are they mostly from rural, urban, or suburban areas?

_____

_____

What do the majority of people in the audience do professionally? Are they entrepreneurs? Small business owners? CPAs? CFAs? Avon reps?

_____

_____

Do most of the members of this audience belong to a certain group, such as a chamber of commerce, business association, or nonprofit organization? If so, what do you know about the characteristics of this organization? What is its mission? Has it experienced growth, or is it in a decline?

_____

_____

What traits do I have in common with this audience?

What is the message I am going to convey to this audience?

What are the main points I need to stress to support this message?

What do I want the audience to say about my speech when it is over?

What do I want the audience to feel about my speech after it concludes?

What do I hope to accomplish with this speech?

These questions are fundamental to ensuring that you have clearly identified your goals and know your audience.

The Mental Game

Part of the reason having conversations with your friends and family is so easy and natural is that you tend to lose yourself in the conversation and enjoy it. You focus on the other person and you stop focusing on yourself. As speakers, however, we tend to do the opposite. We tend to become very self-absorbed while we're on the moon, and we spend more time thinking about what we're saying than we do about how mission control is feeling about what we are saying.

What do you think about while you are giving a speech? If you are one of those people who constantly critiques yourself while speaking, then you aren't thinking about your audience, and you aren't doing your job as a communicator. Remember, communication is a two-way street. Effective public speaking requires you to have a conversation with your audience. While this doesn't necessarily mean the audience members will be doing any of the talking, your focus needs to be on them (and what you are saying in relation to them) and not on yourself. In short, effective public speaking *requires* you to be in the moment and to stop the self-criticism, just like when you are having a conversation with your friends and family. When you stop analyzing yourself and start focusing on your listeners, you will find increased confidence and a greater connection with your audience.

Be Yourself, and Project with Confidence

Many years ago, I had a client who was a very successful lawyer and had decided to run for public office. He never had to do much public speaking in his life before, so he hired me to help him learn, as he put it, to "speak in full sentences." When we started working together, I taught him a technique that he at first laughed at, but which later helped him tremendously. He remains one of my closest friends to this day. Now, this book is not about techniques, but the same thing I taught this gentleman is a great exercise for you to practice to help you speak in public. It's all about proper breathing and projection. See page 88 for details.

Be Yourself, and Know the Room

It's easy for us to be ourselves at Aunt Suzie's house over turkey because we've been to her house so many times that we know it inside and out. Yet the moon is unfamiliar to us and that is why I always recommend that speakers visit the room in which they will give their speech at least once and preferably twice before they have to speak in that room.

One of my clients is a very famous national television personality. We'll call her Robin. Robin is smart, beautiful, talented, wealthy, and before we worked together, she was terrified of public speaking. Even though she is on the news every day in front of millions of people, standing in front of a room and speaking caused her tremendous anxiety. (This is a good reminder that we are not alone in our nervousness.)

Robin was scheduled to present an award at a major awards ceremony at which she would be joined on the stage by very famous celebrities. We practiced her speech quite often, and two days before the event, I met her at the event site, and we practiced her speech on location. Robin stood onstage in front of an empty ballroom that in just a matter of days would hold a few thousand very important people, and she practiced her speech. The key in this exercise is that she was conditioning her mind to believe that speaking in front of this room was familiar. In other words, Robin paid an early visit to the moon so that on the day of the mission, her brain wouldn't be surprised and become anxious. This exercise allowed Robin to visualize herself giving the speech in the exact room where she would actually give it—but we'll cover visualization in more detail in a future chapter.

Visiting the event site ahead of time provides you with a crucial "leg up" in your journey and puts you in the right frame of mind to deliver your speech.

Recently, I met one of my clients at the event site for a speech she was to give later that evening. Even though she rehearsed giving her speech while the banquet staff was setting up the room, just being there and practicing helped her tremendously, and I received a very pleasant thank-you message from her the next day. You guessed it. Her speech had been a success.

Be Yourself and Don't Get Caught off Guard: Do a Mic Check

We usually aren't nervous when we have conversations with our friends and family because there isn't a sound system involved. But the acoustics on the moon are terrible, and the use of a mic is virtually a requirement these days. Given this reality, do yourself a favor and make it easier for you to be yourself by doing a mic check prior to beginning your speech.

Now, I hope you get to the point in your career at which you have a team of advance representatives whose job is to set up the room hours before you arrive to do a thorough check of the sound system. If you are like most people, however, you don't have that luxury. So, here is my advice: arrive fifteen minutes before the start of the event and ask the event coordinator for permission to test the microphone. It's best to check not only the volume but also the position of the mic. Can you remove it from the stand, or is it sealed? Is the height adjustable? These are all good things to know prior to taking command of the podium.

Can Everybody Hear Me?

There are some speakers who think it's great to walk away from a perfectly good sound system and try to fill a packed and large room with their voice. Try to avoid emulating these people. Unless the microphone is defective, my advice is to use it. It provides you with the ability to ensure that everyone in the audience, especially those all the way in the back of mission control, hears you loudly and clearly and feels like you are having a conversation with them versus shouting at them. This does not mean, however, that you need to be held to the confines of the podium. (This is one of the reasons for checking if you can remove the mic from the stand and carry it with you.) Many speakers feel perfectly fine walking out from behind the podium to address the crowd. The choice is yours, but a podium has certain obvious advantages, such as having a great spot to store your speech or note cards. I personally recommend using the podium, especially when you are becoming more comfortable as a speaker.

A Written Speech, Note Cards, or "Just Winging It"

I am often asked whether it is best to write a formal speech, use an outline and note cards, or simply wing it. I am personally not a fan of winging it. However, I don't always recommend writing a formal speech. There are certainly circumstances, however, that call for a formal speech. As a general rule, if you are hired to give a presentation or if you are speaking at a formal event such as a graduation, dinner, or business reception, it is always a good idea to write out a formal speech.

Recently, I worked with a woman who was scheduled to give the keynote speech at a formal charity dinner. The event was honoring the works of a school for autistic children, and she was asked to relate her experiences as a mother of an autistic child whose life had truly been improved by this school. She worked for weeks on her speech and felt compelled to try to memorize it before the event, so it wouldn't look as if she were reading it. My advice to her was simple: Know the material inside and out. Practice the material inside and out. Be able to give the speech without the benefits of having the written speech in front of you. But still make sure you have the speech with you the night of the event, and use it as you would a good tool—refer to it when you need it. It's intimidating being on the moon, and it helps to have something in front of you to reference.

Most professional politicians and corporate executives rely on a teleprompter when giving a speech. In fact, a big part of the work I did when I worked for a state chief executive many years ago was helping him practice his speech—using a teleprompter—for the State of the State address. Although they are extremely helpful, teleprompters can be tricky if you have never used one before, and my recommendation is that you always practice with one before actually using one during your speech.

Most of us, however, will not be fortunate enough to use a teleprompter, so we want to give ourselves every advantage possible by using other methods of preparation.

If you prefer the use of note cards or an outline to a written speech, that is fine. Whatever your preference, follow these simple rules to ensure your success:

- Use at least fourteen-point text if you are typing the speech or notes. I recommend sixteen- to eighteen-point text, because the lighting over the podium is often poor.
- Always write your notes in the order in which you are going to be speaking.
- Always number your cards or the pages of your speech, so that if you should lose your train of thought or drop your cards, you can easily go back to the correct page or note card.
- When you finish speaking from a page, move it to the left of the speech, faceup. Never turn the page facedown. This is to ensure you can easily backtrack if you lose your place in the event that the mic goes out, the power goes out, a waiter drops a tray of dishes, or any other distraction occurs.
- If you are using note cards, buy oversized note cards as opposed to smaller ones.
- If you know your material inside and out because you have practiced, you won't have to worry about appearing as if you are reading the speech. However, there are circumstances in which we suddenly are yanked from the comfort of mission control and asked to quickly

go to the moon with absolutely no preparation. This is when we have to "wing it."

Wing it Effectively by Being Yourself

There is nothing wrong with admitting to your audience that you do not have a formal speech prepared, provided you were not *supposed* to have a formal speech prepared. Remember, the members of mission control are rooting for you and want to see you succeed. Be honest with them and let them know that you do not have the benefit of a prepared speech. When you find yourself in this situation, following Principle 1 is especially vital to success.

First, do not make the mistake of assuming you have to morph into a professional speaker. If you are asked to stand up and give an impromptu speech, speak from the heart, be yourself, and remember you are only having a conversation with your audience. Do not try to be anything other than who you are. Speak the best you can with the information you have at your disposal, and follow these rules of the road:

- Involve mission control. Sometimes the audience members get a little jealous that you get to be on the moon and they are stuck in their seats. So involve them. Ask them questions, and ask the person who is answering to stand up and clearly state his or her name prior to responding. The person will enjoy the attention you have just showered upon him or her.
- Don't apologize for not having a formal speech. Your audience will cut you tremendous slack for having been sent to the moon with little advance warning.

- Begin by speaking about a topic that is familiar to you. Since gaining credibility with an audience usually begins by letting them know who are you and what your background is, you can gain this credibility by starting off with a topic that is familiar to you.
- Unless you have tested the material first, don't make a joke or tell a funny story simply because you are nervous and trying to break the ice. You might break a lot more than just ice.
- Don't feel you have to speak for a long period of time, particularly if you have had little advance warning. Make your stay on the moon brief. Mission control will expect nothing more from you.
- Thank the audience for allowing you the opportunity to speak. Let mission control know that you view it as a privilege, not a burden.

Once you complete your training and master the 7 Principles of Public Speaking, you will be prepared to handle any speech, extemporaneous or not. You will be ready should you arrive at the event and realize you left your speech in your other coat pocket back at your office an hour away. You will be prepared for anything.

Be Yourself, but Never Offend

It's easy to be lighthearted and funny at the family dinner because you know everyone and you would never tell a joke that would offend your dear Aunt Suzie. But on the moon, we tend to go over the line sometimes, either out of nervousness or because we think we are hosting a Friars Club Roast when we are really just supposed to give a speech. Be yourself, but follow this standard: if it wouldn't be acceptable to use this line at Aunt Suzie's, it isn't appropriate to use it during a speech.

To Joke or Not to Joke? Should We Use Humor in Our Presentations? (Ignore this message at your own risk.)

I am constantly asked if it is important to open a speech with a joke. Some speakers believe a good joke can work wonders to loosen up a crowd and make the speaker more comfortable. While this can be true, a wise speaker will approach humor with caution because as much as a humorous story can help a speech, it can also fall flat and actually hurt a speech—not to mention make your audience incredibly uncomfortable. During a recent election, someone told a racial joke directed at one of the candidates in the race. Of course, the joke fell flat and the speaker became the well-deserved subject of massive national criticism. It was distasteful and wrong and should serve as a strong reminder to all speakers of the need for care in injecting humor into speeches. Jokes that concern race, sex, or religion, or involve foul language, have no place in public communication. They can ruin an evening. Unless you are a highly trained professional paid to speak at a Friars Club Roast (see page 50), leave the questionable humor to the comedians.

Here are some thoughts to consider when thinking of using humor in a presentation:

1. Be wary of ever telling a joke simply to tell a joke. Humor should always have a purpose. Although many speakers enjoy using humorous stories, never feel you have to tell a joke or humorous story to warm up an audience. With preparation, visualization, and practice, you can achieve the same level of relaxation and rapport with your audience without employing humor. In other words, don't use humor as a crutch.

2. If you do use a humorous story, test the story before you include it in your speech. Practice the story or joke in front of your friends or family, or videotape yourself to make sure you get the timing right. Remember, professional stand-up comics try out their material at comedy clubs before they go on the *Tonight Show*.

3. If you do tell a joke—and I cannot stress this enough— it absolutely must be G-rated and absolutely must not insult anyone in your audience. If you think a joke might be offensive, it most likely will be, and you should omit it. If you think a joke might hurt someone's feelings, it probably will, and you should discard it. And if you think a joke might be misinterpreted, it probably will be, and you should lose it.

4. Not all occasions call for a humorous story. Know your audience. Do your research, and be prepared. A joke or humorous anecdote may not be appropriate given the crowd and subject matter, and if you are unsure, err on the side of caution, and put the joke or story aside for another day.

5. Remember Principle 6 of the 7 Principles of Public Speaking training program: "Speak to Serve." This

principle teaches us that our role as a speaker is one of service, and our job as a speaker is to serve the audience by sharing, connecting, and making the presentation interesting.

Be Yourself, and Make an Introduction

Have you ever watched the Friars Club Roast? It is a really hysterical comic event during which some of the greatest comic minds come together to roast someone famous. They take turns at the podium shredding the reputation of the guest of honor, who laughs hysterically, and then they spend the last few moments of the roast saying how great the person is.

Similar to the roast, at the White House Correspondents' Association Dinner, reporters and comedians make jokes at the expense of the president of the United States ... who is sitting right there. And the president goes up to the podium and gives it right back to the members of the press association.

These events are hilarious undertakings, but unless the event where you are called to introduce a speaker or serve as master of ceremonies falls into either of these two categories, you need to tread very carefully when making jokes at the expense of other people.

When you are asked to serve as the master of ceremonies for an event, it is crucial that you not offend the organization that invited you or the individual you are asked to introduce. This may seem like common sense, but you would be surprised by the number of people who think that it is acceptable to make jokes at other people's expense when serving as master of ceremonies. If you are asked to introduce someone of honor and you want to make a joke at his or her expense, please do yourself a favor and clear it with both the individual and the organization.

There are also certain general rules to remember when making introductions. When there are important people in the room whom you will be introducing or recognizing, it is always critical that you know how to pronounce their names and correct titles. It is simply not enough to read the names that someone gives you. Take the time to review the names. Make sure they are spelled correctly, that their titles are correct, and that you can easily pronounce both names and titles. And make sure no one is forgotten.

I have seen far too many political events at which an important person, such as a member of congress or a major political donor, did not make it onto the recognition list. The omission caused hard feelings and made the speaker feel very uncomfortable.

To avoid this embarrassing situation, make sure you ask for the guest list ahead of time. Review the list with the event coordinator to ensure that everyone of importance is included in the introductions. If you have questions about a person whom you feel should be introduced, play it safe and ask the event organizer. As the speaker, you are responsible for getting this information correct.

Unless you are advised otherwise, it is also important that you thank the event host, organizers, staff, and any volunteers for their hard work. I have seen speakers who make it a point to thank the waitstaff and chefs if the event is held at a restaurant or banquet room. This is an excellent practice to implement.

Some event organizers may not want you to thank the staff, and that is something to work out well ahead of time. Simply put, as the master of ceremonies, you are the ambassador between the event and the audience, and good communication between the two parties is essential to ensuring the evening goes off without a hitch.

Principles in Action

For the Team

Break the team into groups of three. Ask each team member, while seated, to have a basic conversation with two other team members. In that conversation, have the team members take turns speaking about what they do and a past achievement they are proud of.

Reassemble the entire team, and have each person stand up and re-create the exact conversation that just occurred in the group settings, only this time, have the member stand in front of the whole group. Remind the members that there is no difference between having the conversation with three people while they were sitting down versus having the conversation with the entire team while they are standing.

For the Executive

Remember to always be yourself in a small-group situation. Audiences will appreciate you if you are "just like them," so make it your goal to come across as naturally as you possibly can. Get over trying to sound like a "CEO." The most successful CEOs in the world are able to relate to an audience. Otherwise they wouldn't be successful in the first place!

PRINCIPLE
PERFECTION 2

When You Make a Mistake,

No One Cares but You

" While one person hesitates because he feels inferior, the other is busy making mistakes and becoming superior. "

—Henry C. Link

PERFECTION

Recently, I was at a charity dinner when a gentleman walked over to me and said, "I need to talk to you. I understand that you're a public speaking coach, right?"

I told him I was and asked him what I could do to help.

He looked me straight in the eye and said, "I'm terrified of public speaking. I can't give a speech, and I'm terrified. I can't get up in front of people and speak at all."

I said, "Okay. That's kind of common."

He said, "No, you don't understand. I don't even go to family functions just in case I have to give a speech. I won't go to baptisms. I won't go to christenings. I won't go to Thanksgiving. I won't even go to Christmas dinner, because if somebody asks me to give a toast, I won't know what to do. I haven't gone to a wedding in years. I haven't gone to a family reunion … "

"Stop right there," I said, "I don't know if I'm the right person to talk to. You might need a psychiatrist, but let's try to break this down a little bit. What are you so afraid of?"

He said, "I'm afraid I'm going to make a mistake and everyone in the room is going to think I'm a total idiot."

That is unfortunate, because fear robs us of so much in life. It takes away the fun and the joy, and I believe that the reason so many people are afraid of public speaking is that they are afraid of making a mistake.

As with so many of my examples of public figures, whether you agree with their politics or not, we can all learn a great deal from women and men who hold high public office. They have to speak all the time, so they are constantly refining their skills.

The year was 1981, and the new president of the United States of America, Ronald Reagan, was dealing with bringing the economy back from the highest levels of inflation and economic instability the nation had experienced in years. Those who grew up in that era remember long lines at the gas pumps, a fuel embargo, and a federal budget that was massive. Taxes were high. Consumer confidence was low. The new president had asked the nation a question during the campaign: "Are you better off today than you were four years ago?" Voters answered no and elected him in a landslide. Now he had to deliver and turn the economy around.

In Reagan's mind, the solution would only appear once the federal budget—which had grown at record levels in the 1970s—was dramatically slashed. But before he could cut the budget, he needed Congress to approve his plan, and that meant first getting the American people on board. At his 1981 State of the Union Address, the president dropped the large, bound federal budget on the lectern to the laughs of the audience. The physical demonstration proved the point and told a powerful story of a government that had grown. But that speech wasn't enough. The president knew he would have to spend months working to convince the public of his idea. So he began delivering a series of radio addresses to explain his ideas.

Ronald Reagan is commonly referred to as the Great Communicator. But during the course of one of his radio addresses—when he was talking about the painful cuts that needed to happen for the economy to rebound during what was probably one of the most important moments of his young presidency; when he was laying the groundwork for a reluctant Congress to approve a budget plan that meant so many cuts; when the American public was expecting this man to deliver so they would stop hurting—Ronald Reagan, the Great Communicator himself, made a mistake.

He stumbled on a word. Just as so many speakers do each and every day.

And I bet you are wondering just what he did at that moment.

He could have stopped the speech mid-sentence. He could have changed his delivery as self-doubt spiraled in his mind. He could have allowed himself to be thrown off his game. He could have done any number of those things.

Instead, he kept going.

(After all that buildup I bet you are dying to know what the word was that he stumbled over. Truthfully, I don't remember—and neither will your audience when you stumble on a word.)

The Great Communicator made a mistake and he kept going. And this brings me to my question: If Ronald Reagan, the fortieth president of the United States—a man to whom historians refer as the Great Communicator, a man who had to speak in front of millions of people on a weekly basis, and a man who was a professionally trained actor—can make a mistake, why can't you?

Yet, for so many of us, the idea of making a mistake fills us with anxiety, creates doubt in our abilities, and causes us to hold back our potential instead of unleashing it.

What is the mistake you fear the most when speaking in public, and how do you think making this mistake would affect you?

Now, many people would say that the mistake they fear is that they'll get up in front of the microphone and will just blank out and won't know what to say. They fear that they will completely freeze up and everyone will just stare at them. Some people answer that they're afraid that they will get up to the podium and will start stuttering their words and won't be able to make a full sentence. Other people fear that they will walk up to the podium, trip, and everyone will laugh at them.

Some people even fear they are going to get a fact wrong and it will cost them their entire career.

I mentioned to you earlier that public speaking is largely a mental game and overcoming fears and these anxieties is crucial to success. If you are a beginner, understanding this is the first step on your own journey toward becoming an effective communicator. If you are an experienced speaker, then this is the time in your career when you may fear making a mistake more than ever before simply because the stakes are now higher.

Luke's Story

Meet Luke.

Luke had everything going for him. Smart, talented, and in his mid-thirties, he was promoted as a regional sales manager for one of the most powerful and profitable radio companies in the United States. He oversaw a strong sales team from three different states, and the team's combined sales success stretched into the millions.

His team was performing. Profits were soaring. Management was happy.

Yet, Luke could not confidently deliver the great news about his team's success. So he called me, and we went to lunch. During the course of the conversation, I began to realize that Luke was afraid that if he made a factual mistake, he would lose all credibility in the eyes of management and lose his position.

Maybe. Maybe not.

My prescription to Luke was simple: Make sure you have your facts right. I thought that would be the end of it, but I was mistaken.

Luke held back. He didn't take the risks necessary to become a truly effective communicator. Even with his facts in order, he was terrified of making a mistake and losing credibility in the eyes of management.

Imagine if Reagan, when he made a mistake, had felt the same way that Luke did.

Now, consider a second question. We've already figured the mistake you most fear while public speaking. Now, I want you to write the answer to this: What do you believe the audience *thinks* when you make that mistake?

Many people write that they think that the audience will just start laughing at them, that there would just be laughter all throughout the auditorium, and that the laughter wouldn't stop for hours. I have to admit to you that this would make me terrified of giving a speech, too! If I really thought this would happen, I would never get behind a podium! Actually, I probably wouldn't leave the house!

Now, I'd like you to do one more exercise for me, and then we're really going to get to the root of this principle. Please write down the names of three public speakers who have never made a mistake while speaking in public in their entire speaking careers.

Of course you know already that you will never be able to write down three names.

Note that the principle we're talking about is called, "When you make a mistake, no one cares but you." It's not called, "*If* you make a mistake, no one cares but you." That's because even the most accomplished public speaker will, at times, make a mistake. The important thing to remember is that no one cares but you.

No one cares? *Really?*

Yes, really. No one cares. Odds are that they don't even know you made a mistake.

People's attention spans constantly wander. In fact, most people only absorb about 20 percent of a speaker's message.

They visually internalize the other 80 percent. This ratio is true in nearly everything from a football game or your favorite television show to a heart-to-heart conversation.

Think for a moment about your own life. How many times this past week have you caught your mind wandering? When was the last time you were actually concentrating so intently on driving your car that you didn't have one hand on the radio dial, the other hand holding a cup of coffee, and you only changed positions to shift gears—all the while carrying on a conversation? All of us have minds that wander. It's a natural human tendency, and it is especially true when our only cues are verbal—for example, when reading a book about public speaking (even one as imaginative and entertaining as this!).

Please answer honestly for me: How many times has your mind wandered since you started reading this book? And I won't feel bad about it. The reality is that you don't have moving pictures in front of you or flashing lights and loud music to keep your attention focused. Think about how much money Hollywood filmmakers spend to ensure that big action movies are so over the top that audiences are glued to their chairs for an hour and a half. They spend millions and millions of dollars.

Unfortunately, this means that I have some bad news for you: You are not more interesting than somebody's favorite movie.

But I also have good news for you: You are not more interesting than someone's favorite movie!

Once you understand this, you will be free to make mistakes, and with that freedom comes effectiveness. Now, this is an incredibly important step to master if you truly want to become an effective communicator. Let's face it, when you're up at the podium, you are going to mess up on a word. Your mind may actually go blank for a few seconds, but your mind is never going to go blank to the point that you can't talk about something, and you're never going to mess up to the point where you can't recover and start talking again. The audience is never going to start laughing at you from room to room. It's just not going to happen.

These are unrealistic fears that we as speakers must overcome.

Every time I give a speech, I get nervous just like every single person out there who has to give a speech, but I have learned to channel this nervous energy and use it to give me energy and confidence out there. This allows me to connect with my audience, and it's a great feeling! But I don't sit backstage before I go out to speak and constantly ask myself, "What if I mess up? What if I make a mistake? What if I stumble on my words? What if I forget one of the principles? What if the audience laughs? What if I see somebody checking his or her BlackBerry in the front row and it distracts me?" I don't focus on these things, because all of them will probably happen at one time or another. But if I spend my time focusing on them, I will not feel confident and will not be an effective communicator.

And guess what? The same is true for you. You won't be an effective communicator if all you've done backstage is think about how everything can go wrong for you. That's not a good mind-set to have when you walk out in front of an audience.

Effective communicators understand that mistakes happen, and it's okay!

So, in reality, Principle 2, just like Principle 1, basically means that you have to be yourself. You would never avoid having a conversation with your wife, husband, coworker, son, or daughter because you were afraid of making a mistake during the course of the conversation. So, please don't be afraid to make a mistake when talking to more than one person. Remember, Principle 1 says stop trying to be a great public speaker. Just be yourself. Public speaking is simply what happens whenever you're talking to more than one person. So, get over the idea that you have to be in front of a podium with lights and press and audience members there and that you have to be perfect, because even the people who are out there on that stage with lights and the press and the audience members make mistakes.

Whether you are the president of the United States or a public speaking coach just like me, you will make mistakes. It's part of being human. And this humanity is what makes us great public speakers in the end, because it enables us to connect with our audience. As members of an audience, we don't want to hear perfection. We want to hear from someone who is just like us, and we're all human beings. We're all fallible. So, when you make a mistake, no one cares but you. Remember this, and you will be on your way to overcoming fear and becoming a truly effective communicator.

From Theory to Practice: Making It Work

Annette is one of my favorite clients ever. When I first met her, I thought she was cold and unfriendly, but over time I realized she has a heart the size of a small city and a love for other people that taught me great lessons.

Yet, as a woman who succeeded in corporate America, she had taught herself to put on a very tough veneer, an outer shell to protect her from rejection. Throughout forty years in business, she amassed success and a fortune to go along with it. Some of my favorite days were spent at her seaside resort in a house that was worth somewhere in the ballpark of $25 million. And Annette came from nothing.

We met because she wanted to run for public office and was advised that her hard exterior would not position her as the best candidate. Voters tend to like candidates who are warm and fuzzy, which is why so many political candidates hire advisors to help them figure out every aspect of their style, from their dress to their speech.

Annette hired me to teach her public speaking.

Her first few speeches were cold. She had a hard time opening up, and she treated questions as an inquisition. That may work in the company boardroom, but it won't work at the county fair. Annette needed to change her perspective and approach, but I sensed that she was holding back for some reason I couldn't quite grasp.

I asked her if she would do me a favor and allow me to try a little exercise with her. During one of our training sessions, I asked her staff to leave the room and I asked her to tell me about herself. I didn't want to hear her carefully constructed stump speech prepared by her speechwriters. I wanted to hear about her life, about who she is and where she came from.

That was not an easy prescription. In fact, we started arguing as she kept questioning what this had to do with her winning the election.

Finally, I persuaded her to tell me about herself, her parents, her life.

And then the floodgates opened.

Annette began to explain how her parents abandoned her as a child and she was raised by her grandfather, a man of very modest means who taught her incredible life lessons about hard work and responsibility. A man who taught her to understand her faith and her relationship to God. A man who, for all intents and purposes, was the only parent she ever knew.

And then there she was, standing in my office, a multimillionaire captain of industry, weeping as she told me how scared she had felt all these years trying to live up to the expectations placed on her.

I was speechless.

At that moment, an amazing transformation took place. The cold, hard exterior that prevented Annette from forming a true connection with her audience melted away, and the warm, caring human being that she truly was emerged.

Whereas in the past Annette had been a very hard person to warm up to, soon thereafter, on the campaign trail, reports came in that she was having great conversations with voters. Her speaking took off, and she soon discovered great wit and a gift for empathizing with the struggles her would-be constituents faced.

What had changed?

One day, after Annette had held her official campaign kick-off and her closest advisors all commented on how much she had improved, we had a chance to talk, student to coach. I asked her to what she attributed the change, and she told me in words I will never forget:

"I remember what Grandpa used to tell me about making mistakes: 'If you don't make mistakes, you will never grow.' I was so afraid of making a mistake up there, and then I realized that if I didn't take the risk, I would never win this election."

I won't tell you what the outcome of the election was, but I will tell you that as a speaker, Annette was never the same. She had improved dramatically and experienced renewed growth as a human being.

I've said before that there is something almost magical about making connections with other people through communication. It seems so obvious, yet I fear true communication between people is starting to suffer in the age of BlackBerrys and cell phones.

This point was driven home to me the other night when I saw a couple having dinner together and both of them were on their BlackBerrys. That's not to say those tools aren't important, but when true communication occurs, it is very special. If you are afraid of making a mistake, this principle should serve as your wake-up call that it is only by allowing yourself to make mistakes that you will grow both as a speaker and as a person. By removing your armor, as Annette did, you will unleash your potential.

Shifting Attention Spans

As a speaker, you are competing with real life, and the demands of real life are intense. Unlike going to a movie, when people consciously choose to walk into a theater and forget about life for ninety minutes, most people who come to hear a speech are extremely aware of the world around them, and they are waiting—sometimes patiently, sometimes not—for the speech to end so they can rejoin that world. Your job as a speaker is to remember this and do your best to draw them into your speech.

There was a great line from a Hollywood director who once said, "If they take their eyes off the screen you've lost them." He was giving a modern variation on William Shakespeare's concept of the willing suspension of disbelief. In movies, the minute the audience stops to say, "This is just a movie," the disbelief becomes real and the connection between audience and screen is broken.

Common "disbelief" thoughts include things such as: "Come on, that can't happen; that's so unrealistic," "I wonder how much that explosion cost," "That is a stuntman, no way that's the star," or "That was the corniest line I've ever heard."

When the audience thinks these thoughts during the movie, you can be sure the movie isn't going to be winning too many awards.

And once the connection is broken, it is virtually impossible to repair.

The same is true with public speaking. The minute the audience members start to think, "This speech is going on

too long," or "This guy is so monotonous," or "What time do they serve lunch?" they've stopped listening to you, and your connection with them is broken. Your job is to be aware of this and work to win the attention struggle. Think of it as a game of tug-of-war.

On one side you have the speaker pulling the audience toward the speech, and on the other side, you have the demands of the world and people's natural, limited attention spans. Now, imagine that above the attention span, the "tug," are words like:

- Bills
- College tuition
- Angry boss
- Car repair
- Weekend getaway
- Starving
- BlackBerry

These are the things that give fuel to the other side, making your job to keep the tug alive and in balance require that much more work and attention.

Most speakers think that they'll rein in their listeners with slides and pictures (and we'll discuss these tools in depth), but the key to remember is that audience attention usually comes in waves. That is to say, it's not so much that the audience is with you for a while and then you lose them for the remainder of the speech. Rather, people will be with you for a few minutes, then their attention will wander for thirty seconds or so, and then it may come back, or it may continue to wander. But people will usually check in and check out. As speakers, if we think creatively about how to keep bringing people back into focus, we'll do our job.

First of all, never be the kind of speaker who gets angry at the audience members for his own inability to keep them interested. I've heard speakers use demeaning tones and say things like:

"Come on, people, stay with me," "What, does this crowd have ADD or something?" or "Look, this is important, pay attention."

I know one thing: Those speakers have never received a standing ovation. They have not only broken the connection with their audience but also have most likely created a hostile audience that is not going to care one iota about what they have to say. There is no quicker way to lose your listeners than to insult their intelligence.

Respect your audience members' attention, and never belittle them. It's not their fault that this tug exists; it's natural. Hollywood has special effects and thematic music on its side to win the struggle. All you have is your speech. (Even if you wanted to use special effects, you could never compete with Hollywood.)

So it's your job to pull your listeners in and keep the tug-of-war in balance.

How do we do it?

Eye Contact

A good speaker will never read a speech. This sounds like common sense, but even people who wind up making note cards often fall back on reading those cards because of the security they afford. Looking into other people's eyes may seem intimidating, but it is not. It's something you do every single day when you are having conversations with people one-on-one. So why should adding a few more eyes to the mix be intimidating?

The truth is we make it intimidating because we are not used to it, but by consciously remembering that in our culture eye contact is a normal part of human interaction and something we do every time we have a conversation, we should have no problem doing it during a speech. In reality, public speaking is nothing more than having a conversation.

Here is where Principles 1 and 2 begin to intersect. Eye contact has the direct effect of signaling to someone, "I should pay attention here; someone is talking to me." It also makes people feel important and makes them feel like you care about them. And they are much more likely to put all their worries on hold and focus on you for a few more minutes if they believe you care about them.

Many years ago, a public speaking coach gave bad advice to clients who were nervous about eye contact. He told them to pick a spot on the back of the wall that is right above the audience members' heads, such as a clock, and look at that to give the audience members the *feeling* that you are speaking to them. Gimmicks such as this do not work, and audiences are too smart to fall for them. If you take the bad advice this coach gave, your listeners are going to wonder why you keep looking over their heads, and they will tune you out faster than they would a bad commercial during their favorite Thursday-night television show.

Another gimmick often used by coaches consists of advising people to look at the audience's foreheads to give the illusion you are making eye contact with them. All this will do is leave the audience members wondering if they somehow managed to get part of their lunch on their face or if they have really bad dandruff. Don't fall back on gimmicks. They never work.

Good public speaking is all about having that conversation with the audience. Good speakers are not afraid to look other people in the eye.

Tone & Pitch

Tone of voice and vocal emphasis are also essential to keeping this struggle in balance. Good speakers will write their remarks in a way that occasionally throws in phrases designed for vocal inflection, because when the audience hears the speaker's tone of voice shift, it is an automatic verbal cue to pay attention. If a speaker drones on and on about tax laws and all of a sudden says the room is on fire in the same tone of voice, only those smelling the smoke will pay attention. But if the speaker delivers the fire warning in the way it should be delivered—with urgency and inflection—you can bet everybody will wake up and call the fire department.

So while you should never yell "fire" in a crowded auditorium, you should write lines that cause your voice naturally to go up, and you should also write lines that cause your voice to go down, even to the point of becoming quiet. Believe it or not, when you lower the tone of your voice, it actually causes people to listen and tune in just as effectively as if you were to shout something. Plus, it's a whole lot more respectful than yelling at your audience.

So how do you write these inflection lines?

Think about places within your remarks that would allow such entries. For example, if you are giving a speech about tax law, throw this line in after a particularly boring paragraph about changes to the tax code:

"But the GOOD NEWS, everyone, is that this means substantial (dramatic pause) savings … for all of us!"

Or perhaps this line: "But guess what, friends, (dramatic pause) this means we are all … going … to … pay a little more this year. I know, I know. This is not my favorite part of the speech."

Lines like these will bring the audience back into focus, and it will do so in a way that causes your listeners to like you much more than if you scolded them for tuning you out for a few moments.

Good speakers take the necessary time to plan such lines throughout their speeches.

Action Steps: Creating Your Key Lines

As you work on your material, think about the benefits you are offering your audience as well as any potential downside to what you are saying. Write both down in a column, just like in the example on the next page.

All of these advantages and disadvantages can be used to bring the audience's attention over to your side of the tug. As you write your speech, think creatively of where these remarks should go. Remember, people's attention spans go in waves, so they are usually with you at the opening of your speech, especially if you have a strong opening, as we will discuss later. People are also usually with you during the close of your speech because they recognize that all good things must come to an end and you have prepared them in your speech for the imminent closing.

It's usually during the murky middle of the speech that people's minds tend to wander, so try to insert a line that allows your tone of voice to go up or down at least once or twice in every paragraph. This will ensure the audience member stays with you longer rather than focusing on his or her car's need for an oil change.

Benefits	Disadvantages
• Substantial savings to the family	• Increased paperwork
• New exploration of undersea medical cures	• Big expense to the health care industry
• Lower interest rates for homeowners with good credit	• Increased disclosure means harder to get a mortgage today
• New deductions give you more money back for dependents	• The maximum number of dependents you can declare is four

The Dramatic Pause

President Bill Clinton is an artful user of the dramatic pause, and you should be, too. Most speakers tend to think that a dramatic pause is deadly and that the audience will feel the dead air and get antsy. Just the opposite, however, is true. A well-timed dramatic pause has the effect of sending a cue to the listener to tune in, because chances are something good is coming.

Watch Bill Clinton during a press conference. When he is asked a question, he usually pauses for a few seconds, even occasionally looking off as if he is gathering his thoughts, and then gives a very well-considered answer. And because he pauses for a few seconds, the listeners stop thinking of everything else in the world and tune in to hear what he has to say.

A dramatic pause has a number of advantages and should always be a part of your speaker's arsenal.

A well-placed pause:

- Sends a verbal cue to the listener that something important is coming.
- Breaks up the tone of voice, allowing the ear to recognize new vocal pitch.
- Causes the audience to think that the speaker really has his or her thoughts together.
- Is good theater and is a technique used all the time in quality drama by great actors and public figures.
- Will always feel longer to the speaker than to the audience. So don't rush it. You will be more aware of its length than your listeners will, as they are focused not on the pause, but on your next words.

There are also things you can do to make sure your speech is going to be comfortable for everyone. Anyone who attends a taping of the *Late Show with David Letterman* is advised to bring a light jacket or sweater, even during a hot New York summer. That's because Dave keeps the temperature in the Ed Sullivan Theater in the 60s. Why? So people don't fall asleep! A theater or venue that is too hot will make it more difficult for you as a speaker to rein your audience in. That doesn't mean that you can always control the temperature, but you can try.

Ask the event coordinator about the temperature and see if you can get to the event early to make adjustments if necessary. Remember, people's normal body temperature is approximately 98 degrees, so a group of people will cause a room to heat up very quickly. Adjust for that. I always recommend that venues keep the temperature around 68 degrees. This will leave room for the audience's natural body heat to warm up the venue without it becoming uncomfortable.

Particularly in the winter—when many venue coordinators come in from the cold and jack up the heat while they are still freezing—it is important to keep in mind how quickly a roomful of a hundred people will warm up. So take this into account.

Returning to this chapter's opening concept—that when you make a mistake, no one cares but you—remember the following:

If you are onstage and you make a mistake, such as fumbling on a word, keep going. Chances are the audience didn't notice because of the reality of shifting attention spans. The odds that your listeners were really with you, right at that moment, and that they caught your mishap are slim anyway. But even if they did notice, so what? As we've discussed earlier, they aren't going to start laughing at you, and you will be able to recover. So keep going.

If you are an experienced speaker and recognize that it is time to take your expertise to the next level, but you are afraid of making a mistake, ask yourself a few questions:

What is holding me back as a speaker?

What could I accomplish if I didn't hold back?

_____

If I don't hold back and I make a mistake, what's the worst that will happen?

_____

What is the reality that this "worst-case scenario" will really happen?

_____

If it does happen, what will that mean?

_____

After answering these questions, write a positive affirmation for you to reread and study on a daily basis. For example:

It's okay if I make mistakes during a speech. Even the most polished speakers in the world make mistakes from time to time. I'm only human, and part of being a good speaker is having a simple conversation with the audience. I would never avoid having a one-on-one conversation with someone because I fear making a mistake, so I'm not going to fear making a mistake when I'm talking to more than one person.

You now have powerful tools in your speaker's arsenal to keep the attention tug-of-war in balance, overcome your fear of making mistakes, and to remove any limitations that hold you back from being the speaker you have the potential to be.

You have the tools to unleash your potential, overcome your fears, and get the results you've always imagined.

Now it is up to you to put them to work for you.

PRINCIPLE 3
VISUALIZATION

If You Can See It, You Can Speak It

> **The human brain starts working the moment you're born and never stops until you stand up to speak in public.**
>
> —Anonymous

VISUALIZATION

Our brain is really amazing. To comprehend its powers—to understand that it is more powerful than any computer ever invented; to recognize that the human brain is responsible for space travel, skyscrapers, nuclear weapons, and more; to grasp the brain's endless capabilities—has to give you great pause.

And yet, despite their incredible capabilities, our brains need a tremendous amount of training. Usually, the brain has to experience something several times before it begins to sink in. Think about how many times you have to see a commercial before you actually consider buying the product. Most marketing experts know that there must be at least nine to twelve points of contact before a consumer will feel comfortable reaching into his or her pocket and handing over hard money. Our minds love familiarity, and that is why we usually tend to feel very good about places or smells that give us that nostalgic feeling. How many times have you smelled the scent of homemade cookies and just felt happy? On weekends, do you like going to your usual breakfast place or visiting the neighborhood tavern where "everybody knows your name?"

If you are like me, the answers to the above questions are "many" and "yes," and this is because your brain, like mine, likes to feel comfortable. This principle, however, goes both ways, and it also explains why we feel just a pinch of anxiety when we are in a new place or why we experience dread when we are lost and without the benefit of our navigation systems.

We like to do the things we do every day. And typically, we don't have to give a speech every day.

As incredible as our brains are, they have to be trained, and we have to be taught. Our brains are capable of designing skyscrapers, but we're not born with the blueprints buried in our subconscious minds. We have to learn how to design. A great brain surgeon can remove life-threatening tumors, but we want that surgeon to go through years of medical school and even more years of on-the-job training before putting a scalpel to our heads.

Let's face it: we're not born great doctors, great lawyers, great musicians, or great actors. We may be born with a natural potential for these talents, but it takes a tremendous amount of training to bring this potential front and center.

The same is true with public speaking.

The moment that we begin to get out of our chair and stand up in front of a group often fills our hearts and minds with anxiety. Why? Because we are stepping into a scenario to which our brains are not accustomed.

In Principle 1, we clearly established that to be a truly effective communicator, all you have to do is learn to speak like yourself—to approach public speaking as a conversation with the audience rather than as a "speech."

Yet, when we begin to rise out of our chairs to have that conversation, anxiety enters the picture because our brains are not used to us standing in front of people and speaking. Our brains are used to us talking to other people while we are sitting or while we are talking on the telephone. In fact, most people don't feel anxiety when they are giving a presentation that requires them to remain seated. They report their anxiety level is much less before, during, and after the speech than when they have to deliver the exact same presentation to the exact same audience while standing up.

Again, it's time for a paradigm shift in our thinking about public speaking, and this shift specifically addresses how to overcome the so-called fear of public speaking.

I'm going to throw an idea out to you, and please give me a chance to explain it before you conclude that I'm crazy. A lot of people give me reasons they are "afraid" of public speaking. Some say it is because they are afraid of looking like an idiot or making a fool out of themselves. Some report that they don't feel prepared and fear losing credibility. All of these thoughts are important to flesh out, and we will do that more throughout the course of the book. But I'm still not convinced that these are the *real* reasons that public speaking consistently ranks as people's greatest fear.

I believe the reason so many people really "fear" public speaking is that the experience of standing in front of a roomful of people who are seated is unfamiliar territory for our brains, and this creates the feeling of anxiety. Simply put, our brains are not accustomed to this environment, and much as with being lost or entering a strange place for the first time, our immediate mental reaction is, *"This is unfamiliar to me."* This translates into the classic physiological "flight or fight" syndrome that causes us to experience a rush of adrenaline and makes us feel "nervous" and, more often than not, wishful we could "fly" from the room. This is the reason so many people tell me that their anxiety is highest *before* they begin speaking versus during their speech.

As speakers, we need to overcome this anxiety, because even if we are truly gifted speakers, the anxiety can throw us off our game. I know many speaking coaches try to convince their clients that a little anxiety is a good thing. That's one theory, and perhaps there is some truth to it. But I know from personal experience that when you feel confident and not anxious, you tend to perform better. How many world champions do you know who allow themselves to feel anxiety before they compete? I'll be honest: I don't know any. The champions I know work hard to ensure that they feel nothing but confidence before they compete.

I want you to experience that same level of confidence before you speak. I want you to get over the anxiety and walk to the podium clear, focused, and on your game. Forget the butterflies flying in the right direction. Let confidence swat the butterflies away.

And the way to achieve this confidence is to convince your brain that standing in front of a group of people and speaking is as familiar as brushing your teeth—even if you give only one speech a year. The way to do this is to master the same tool that professional athletes use to experience confidence and overcome their physical and mental limitations to achieve greatness—a tool so incredibly advantageous to champions that all of us should be using it in our life: the power of visualization.

But before we dive into this tool, first, a story.

There was a young man who, while growing up, performed in school plays. He loved the feeling of being out on the stage so much that he was often accused of "stealing the show." When he was out there on that stage, in front of a huge crowd, he knew that this was why he was put on this earth. He felt it every time he walked on the stage and every time he finished the performance and received a standing ovation. Talk about understanding your destiny!

But prior to his performance, he would get so physically ill that he would throw up, get migraine headaches, and snap at people. In fact, if you crossed him before he made his entrance to the stage he would probably bite your head off. But before you start accusing this guy of being a total jerk, I should confess that I am the guy. As good as I was once I got out on the stage, and as much as I enjoyed being out there, prior to walking out on stage, I wanted to die. The anxiety was overwhelming. I used to keep rosary beads in my pocket and do nothing but pray to God begging him to let me be okay.

I'm not joking. My anxiety was that bad. I had what psychologists like to call "stage fright." Today, they would probably give me some sort of antianxiety cocktail, but back then I had to rely on the old-fashioned remedies. And it wasn't until I heard a story about basketball great Larry Bird that I understood how I could overcome this fear and unleash my true potential.

A Tale of Two Athletes

Larry Bird was hired to make a car commercial, and in the ad he was supposed to miss a free throw. Legend has it that it took over two dozen takes before Bird was capable of *missing* the shot. That's because he had spent so many years of his life practicing his free throw shot that when he intentionally tried to miss the shot, his mind would autocorrect and adjust the shot, so he would make the basket. He didn't even have to try. Like a spell-checker that automatically fixes a commonly misspelled word, Bird's mind took over and fixed the problem.

That was a result of years of visualization.

In his book *On Winning*, Michael Jordan talks about how he would visualize for hours a day, spending time seeing himself making the shot and winning the game. Even though he played virtually every day, he still spent hours more each week visualizing himself playing. The power of visualization is that intense, and it is that capable of helping all of us reach our true potential.

If world-class athletes Michael Jordan and Larry Bird used this visualization technique to become so effective in a highly competitive field—professional basketball— can we as public speakers use this same tool to overcome fear and anxiety and become effective communicators?

Absolutely.

The fact of the matter is that all great winners in life have something in common: they harness the power of visualization to achieve their goals. Salespeople envision themselves closing the deal. Executives picture themselves developing new ventures. Athletes close their eyes and imagine themselves making that basket, hitting that home run, or breaking that record.

As speakers, we can use this same skill to connect with our audiences.

The best way to fight anxiety and become a more comfortable speaker is to practice in the one place where no one else can see you—the one place that matters the most: your mind.

Visualization works because the mind cannot distinguish between what is real and what is imagined. So, whether you are an experienced speaker looking to take your skills to the next level or a new speaker hoping to overcome fear, visualization will transform your abilities. But it will only work for you if you make the commitment to visualize your speaking success on a regular and consistent basis.

Larry Bird and Michael Jordan didn't decide to use visualization once in a while; they did it every day. It's that level of commitment that made them champions, and it's that level of commitment that will make you an effective communicator.

I'm going to give you a simple exercise to do every night for half an hour. It will not only help your mind get used to giving a speech, but it will also help your body learn to relax and will condition you for the kind of effective breathing necessary to give a speech.

In your house, when no one else is around, turn down the lights and get rid of all distractions. Turn off the radio. Turn off your TV. Turn off your cell phone. Don't just put it on vibrate. Actually turn it off. Close your eyes and begin to breathe comfortably and normally. You may lie down or sit up—whichever you choose. The point is to be comfortable. Let go of your problems and feel yourself relax. Take a deep breath and hold it for a few seconds as you start to relax. Focus on breathing with your lower stomach. Push out the air with your stomach and inhale through your nose. Hold the air in briefly and push out with your stomach again.

This is the kind of deep breathing great performers use before and while they are on stage. When you push the air out with your lower stomach, you are supporting the exhalation, and that is the secret to projecting your voice in the most natural way.

Now, as you begin to relax, picture a dark and empty room. There are rows upon rows of seats, but no one is sitting in them. At the center of the room is a podium with a microphone and a single glass of water. Walk over to the podium, adjust the mic, and make sure it is comfortable. Tap the head of the mic a few times and say "testing." You notice how hot the light is above you. Take a drink of the water, and feel it cool you down under the hot lights. It's really cool, and suddenly the hot lights don't bother you anymore. You feel energized, and you feel ready.

Start talking about anything—your day, the weather, your favorite spot on the beach. Any topic at all. Have a conversation. Relax. Loosen up, and see yourself relaxed and moving around up there. It's not so bad. It's fun. In the front row, you see someone who makes you feel comfortable—perhaps it's your best friend, your loved one, your significant other, your mother-in-law. You see that person. Acknowledge him or her. Introduce him or her to the whole empty room. For example, say "This is my wife." Then talk directly to that person. See yourself in your mind talking directly to him or her. You don't even notice those hot lights anymore. You're just having a conversation. You feel relaxed. You feel natural. You don't even notice that all those seats have filled up, and hundreds of people are watching you have that conversation with that person you care about. But you don't feel anxious. You feel confident. If you feel anxiety start to creep up, push it away. You're a confident speaker having a conversation with one person, and it feels good.

The brain cannot distinguish between this scenario and a real scenario, and as you practice this scenario each night, your mind will become used to the prospect of speaking in public. Pretty soon, you'll find that the idea no longer elicits those same feelings of anxiety and fear that you felt before. If you will commit yourself to doing this visualization exercise every day for about thirty minutes a day, you will overcome your fear of public speaking. It's guaranteed. No one who visualizes feels afraid after doing so because the mind begins to believe that which is visualized. Yes, you are comfortable in this environment. Yes, this is familiar to you.

Right now, so many of us have a great fear of public speaking because we don't do it that often. We don't have to get up in front of people, so our minds aren't used to it. Train your mind. Train your mind to become used to it. Train your mind to focus on it. Train your mind to believe that this feels good and this is a comfortable environment. When you do it enough, and you stand in front of a room, you will feel relaxed and comfortable and confident because your mind is used to it.

The more real you can make your visualization, the better. In other words, if you have to give a speech next week in front of your company board of directors, it's good for you to picture that boardroom as precisely as you can. Picture the paneling. Picture the wood. Picture where the seats are and how high they are. Are there windows? Is there sunlight? Is there natural light, artificial light? The more detail you can visualize, the better. If you can picture the people that you'll be speaking to sitting in those chairs, that's great. And if you can do this, and if you can see yourself in front of that group, in that room, practicing, talking, and giving that speech, then your mind won't know the difference between the real speech and your visualized speech. When the day comes on which you really have to give that speech, you'll stand up there and will feel a sense of relaxation because you've already done this. You've done it in your mind, and that is the secret of champions.

If Michael Jordan can practice a shot over and over in his mind until he gets it right and consequently go down in history as one of the greatest players—maybe *the* greatest player—the sport has ever known, then you can use the same technique in your journey to becoming an effective communicator. Trust me on this. I use this technique all the time, and I am convinced it is the single greatest technique for overcoming the fear of public speaking and unleashing your potential.

As this experience becomes comfortable to you, try giving an entire speech in your mind. Practice new lines and new stories. Leave the comfort of the podium and walk across the stage. Grab the microphone and walk around with it. Field tough questions, and feel yourself handling them with ease. Understand that your mind is getting used to this scenario. It is becoming commonplace for your mind.

That is why you should spend time visualizing yourself getting out of the chair and rising to speak. As you rise up, tell yourself that just because you are standing, nothing—absolutely nothing else—is changing. You are still just having a conversation with the group.

Your mind will agree.

If you are a very experienced speaker, it is important for you to use this exercise to reach the next level of greatness that awaits you. Picture yourself giving a speech to the audience you truly want to speak to one day. Imagine their faces. Perhaps it is your company CEO or the governor of the state. There are no limitations. If you can picture yourself speaking before those people with the kind of effectiveness you desire, you will find that you are not only preparing your mind for that scenario but also actually attracting the reality of that event. We've all heard of the power of attraction, and that is another book for another day, but the point is simple: If you picture with intensity the scenarios you want, your mind has a funny way of making them happen.

Michael Jordan used to visualize himself playing in the world championship before he ever even made the college basketball team. I have heard of hundreds of champions in life who have visualized their way to success, and sadly I've also met many people who have failed at things because, deep down inside, they didn't believe they could succeed in the first place. Therefore, because of their subconscious thoughts, they didn't work hard enough to begin with. If you don't really believe you can achieve something, why bother? It's easier just to watch television.

But we are champions. We understand that the same mind that is capable of sending a man to the moon, constructing a plane that can defy the laws of gravity, or developing cures for diseases can help us unleash our true potential—*if* we do our job and help our mind.

If you are new to public speaking, use visualization to over-come your fears. If you are an experienced speaker, use this powerful tool to connect with audiences like never before. Wherever you are in your speaking journey, make visualization part of your travel map.

From Theory to Practice: Making It Work

For Individual Evaluation

Take a few moments to answer the following questions. Don't be nervous; this isn't a "pass or fail" exam! It's just a tool to help you understand your perceptions about public speaking. Watch for patterns in your answers— you may be surprised at what you find!

What about public speaking makes you nervous or fearful?

_____

_____

What is your first immediate thought when you learn you have to give a speech?

_____

_____

How do you feel before a speech? Emotionally? Physically? What thoughts go through your mind?

_____

_____

How do you feel during the speech?

_____

_____

What benefits do you see in learning to counter the negative thoughts you have about public speaking with more positive thoughts?

Before whom, in terms of audience, would you most like to speak? Whom do you hope to one day see in your audience?

For the Team

Create a pitch scenario for your team. Ask each member of the team to practice giving that pitch to a particular client. Have the team member give that pitch to the client from start to finish, but only in the team member's mind. Give each member of the team different scenarios to practice—such as the client being stubborn, the client being rude, or the client being receptive. Have your team member give that pitch while tailoring it to each scenario; this way each potential client response becomes familiar and real.

For the Executive

Before whom would you like to speak? The CEO? The president of the United States? Potential investors? Determine your desired audience, and then picture yourself giving a speech in front of that person or persons. Don't just say a few words; give an entire ten-minute speech, from start to finish, in front of that visualized audience.

For the Beginner

Visualize yourself giving your speech in front of ten thousand people in a crowded auditorium. Tell yourself before you walk out on stage and during the speech that the size of the crowd doesn't matter. It is only about having a conversation. The size of the crowd is irrelevant. Visualize this scenario, and tell yourself the right kind of accompanying thoughts.

Remember, if you can see it, you can speak it!

PRINCIPLE
DISCIPLINE 4

Practice Makes ~~Perfect~~ Good

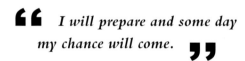 *I will prepare and some day my chance will come.*

—Abraham Lincoln

DISCIPLINE

Please take a moment and name three activities or hobbies that you once did not know how to do but now feel quite comfortable doing. It could be anything—participating in a sport, playing a musical instrument, going to the gym, cooking, making wine, understanding wine. Please write them down.

1. _____

2. _____

3. _____

Now, think about why you enjoy doing them. Do you excel at them because you do them consistently? My guess is that you do these things with passion and that you look forward to doing them. The same thing can happen with public speaking. And if you put into practice the principle in this chapter, you will get the same feeling about public speaking that you have about your hobbies. You will actually look forward to speaking in public!

At the start of our journey together, I mentioned that when I was younger, I was rather shy. Actually, that's an understatement. I used to get the kind of stage fright that would make your palms sweat, and I would get physically sick every time I spoke in front of an audience. To overcome my shyness, I signed up for acting lessons and even performed stand-up comedy for a while. These days, I am in front of an audience all the time either giving speeches or leading training seminars, and I feel very little anxiety before I speak. What changed?

In addition to adopting all of the seven principles throughout the course of my own personal life, I practiced speaking. I practiced a lot. Remember from Principles 1 and 2 that our goal is not to be a perfect public speaker; there's no such thing. Our goal is to be a good public speaker, an effective public speaker, a public speaker who isn't overwhelmed by anxiety and fear, and a public speaker who can connect with an audience. Most important, we should enjoy ourselves when we are in front of an audience. But like anything in life that is worth doing, effective public speaking takes practice.

The Speaker Challenge

Many public speaking books approach practice as an afterthought and not as a fundamental principle. In my years of watching people transform from being "just okay" in front of a group to being truly dynamic, I have discovered that what makes the difference for these speakers is often their level of practice. They have had—and sought out—more opportunities to speak in front of groups. These opportunities are why organizations such as Toastmasters International continue to be effective. They provide an opportunity for individuals to practice their speaking in front of an audience on a consistent basis. Consistency in practice is truly an advantage all great champions share.

But before you can practice effectively, you must invest in an indispensable piece of equipment. It may set you back a few bucks, but I promise it will be money worth spending! What is the equipment? It's called a "full-length mirror," and it is an incredibly effective tool in becoming a better public speaker.

When we do professional training at Richard Zeoli Communications Impact, we utilize not only a mirror but also video analysis. But for individual at-home practice purposes, a basic mirror is the best way to rehearse.

Principles in Action

Stand in front of the mirror and start talking. Don't use any notes; just have a conversation. Watch yourself. How is your posture? What are you doing with your hands? Are you smiling? Now, make a statement about something important, anything, as long as it holds some significance to you. Watch your body language. How did you respond to what you just said? How could you use your hands to help prove your point? Are you smiling? Open up your arms, breathe, and feel comfortable. Remember, you're only talking. You do it every day, so you are naturally capable of doing it and doing it well. It may be uncomfortable at first to stand and watch yourself speak to a mirror, but persist; don't give up. The more you do it, the more natural it will become, and the more natural it becomes, the more people will begin to take notice of you as a good public speaker.

Let's back up to three things that you enjoy doing.

- Up until this point in your life, how has your approach to mastering public speaking been either the same as or different from each of the three activities that you wrote down at the beginning of this chapter?
- Has your level of commitment to public speaking been on par with your commitment to those activities?
- Will you make a commitment to practice in front of a mirror five, ten, or even fifteen minutes a day, every day?
- Select the time amount, and specifically write down your commitment to practicing every single day.

Matt was a very promising up-and-coming salesman who really wanted to improve his speaking in front of groups to increase his sales. I asked Matt once how often he practiced his speaking and his answer, in a word, was "never." But he loved the guitar and told me he usually practiced his guitar three to five nights per week. And he played very well. I am sure that practicing the guitar is fun and incredibly therapeutic, but communication skills are vital to your business success. I am not by any means encouraging Matt or anyone to give up practicing the guitar, as that may yield a similar benefit one day. My point is do both. Treat public speaking practice not as a hobby, but as a necessity for being effective in life. Learn to love it with the same passion that you have for playing guitar, or practicing karate, or doing anything that you love to do.

In the days leading up to a speech, I practice daily. It's important for me to know the material well and to feel comfortable with speaking about the topic. Consider that the world's greatest athletes practice their craft every single day during the regular season, and several days a week during the off-season, and that is why they are the finest athletes in the world.

We would never want the New York Yankees or any professional team to take the field without having gone through spring training. If multimillion-dollar, world-class athletes have to practice, you and I have to practice, too. If you want to become really good, you must mirror their method of success. And truth be told, when you get up in front of that mirror at your house and practice your art and your craft, you will begin to feel more comfortable.

I said earlier that all the principles build on each other. This is a classic example. Just as your mind cannot distinguish between what is actually a speech and what is a visualized speech, when you practice in front of a mirror, your mind becomes accustomed to it, and this helps you become a great public speaker. And the result? When the moment comes when you are in front of the company boardroom or pitching your business to potential customers or speaking at the company dinner with no advance notice, you will be ready.

You will be ready because you've practiced and your mind is ready. Your mind understands how to use your arms without even thinking about it and knows how to make eye contact without concentrating on it.

When I am presenting this principle to an audience, I always like to ask, "How many of you paid attention to your driving on your way to work today? 'Okay, I am going to give 10 percent pressure on the brake pedal and turn my hands 30 degrees to move the wheel, and I am going to look right and then left and then in my rearview mirror and then back to my left.' Who said that?" Nobody! We never do this on the way to work in the morning. We're usually talking on the phone, eating a bagel, or drinking coffee. I actually even saw a guy shaving the other morning while he was driving! Please understand—I do not endorse any of these danger-ous distractions. But the point is clear: We don't consciously think about every single step we take when we're driving our cars because we've done it a thousand times. Our minds recognize what to do and essentially seem to drive the car automatically while we are listening to traffic and weather.

The same can be true of public speaking. If you do it enough, with enough consistency, you will naturally know how to use your hands, your body language, and your voice to maximize your communication. Practicing in front of the mirror every day is a great way to develop this "second-nature" speaking, and you don't even have to talk about anything of significance. Speak about your family vacation. Speak about how much you love your job. Speak about how much you love this book. Just speak!

The Crucial 5s

Do you ever watch the faces of professional athletes prior to the start of the game? I'm fascinated by the looks of intensity in their eyes as they stand on the sidelines waiting for the coin toss or the first pitch. It is a burning desire to win that drives these world-class athletes and virtually ensures that when they take the field, they are stepping out as champions, mentally ready for the intense challenge that lies before them.

This is the same intensity we need to capture as communicators prior to giving a speech.

The five minutes before you are called to the podium or to the front of the boardroom to give your remarks are your most crucial five minutes as a speaker. The Crucial 5s are often the difference between "just okay" and being at the top of your game. Capturing that intensity, that burning desire, is something each one of us must do before we stand on our feet.

How do we do it?

The best way is to mentally picture yourself *successfully* taking the podium and addressing the crowd. In the ideal situation, find a spot alone, backstage, close your eyes and picture the scenario, and tell yourself positive affirmations that will help you succeed. But even if you are sitting in a roomful of people in the company boardroom, you can still achieve this mental advantage. Simply, with your eyes open or closed, picture yourself in front of the room, and tell yourself your specific positive affirmations.

Each of us has unique needs and challenges, so there is no cookie-cutter approach to writing these affirmations. To help you write the most effective affirmations for you, here are a few questions to ask yourself:

How do I feel in the minutes right before I give a speech?

How would I rate my anxiety level on a scale of 1–10, with 10 being most anxious and 1 being not anxious at all?

> What thoughts am I thinking about my own abilities right before I begin?

For many of us, the answer to the first question is usually, "I feel anxious." If this was your answer, then proceed to ask yourself why. Why do I feel anxious? What about getting up to give this speech causes me this anxiety? Depending on your answer, you can craft your personal affirmation statement.

For example, if you wrote, "I am worried that people will think I don't know what I am talking about," then a positive affirmation to tell yourself during The Crucial 5s might be something like this:

I am prepared. I know this material. I know this topic. The audience is going to understand the depth of knowledge and appreciate my subject matter. But I recognize that not 100 percent of the audience will feel this way and that's okay. I am prepared. I am ready.

If your response to the question was, "I am afraid I am going to make a mistake and everyone will laugh at me," then go back to Principle 2 and remember that when you make a mistake, no one cares but you, and tell yourself an affirmation such as:

I am human. Even the world's greatest speakers make mistakes. The audience will appreciate the fact that I am only human and will actually like me more if I am just myself. If I make a mistake, it is okay, because the only person who really cares is me. No one—not my boss, not the audience, not my spouse—expects me to be perfect. I will simply do the best I can do. And that is enough. I am ready.

Or if the answer you gave was something akin to, "I am anxious because this speech means everything to me. If I don't nail it, I won't get the promotion or the customers or the account," then you might want to write an affirmation such as the following:

I am going to give the best possible speech for this moment. I have prepared, and I am ready. I have followed the exercises, and I understand that I am going to be myself and have a conversation with the audience. This is important, and I am ready. I am ready to demonstrate to the audience everything I have learned and the great progress I have made. I am ready.

It is important to practice these affirmations daily and not just in the moments prior to giving a speech. Nevertheless, always repeat them during The Crucial 5s. It is essential to being a truly effective communicator.

Imagine if a starting running back, instead of thinking to himself, "I am a champion," thought things like, "I hope the crowd likes me. What if I drop the ball? What if I miss that catch? Oh no, what happens if I don't make a touchdown? I'll lose my contract, I won't be able to feed my family. I don't want to go out there!"

He probably wouldn't do a very good job during the game.

Yet, for many of us, we think similar thoughts before we get up to give a speech.

I've met people who have admitted to me that before they give a speech, they will think thoughts like these: "I am going to make a mistake." "The audience isn't going to like me." "This topic won't interest the audience." "I'm going to blow it, and I won't get the promotion. I'll lose my business, and my wife will leave me." "I don't want to get up there!"

I cannot stress enough the importance of filling your mind with positive affirmations prior to giving that speech. Even if you are the most experienced and successful speaker in the world, you need to do this exercise. Actually, the most successful speakers in the world already do this exercise. Just ask them.

Sharon's Story

Sharon is smart and beautiful. She is a national television personality and was chosen by her network to fly to Europe to be the master of ceremonies for the international launch of the network's European channel. And yet, even though Sharon is on television daily and has been featured on the cover of major magazines, her anxiety level prior to giving her European speech was a solid 10. Probably higher.

So, she came to see me.

She told me that she was contemplating taking medication for her anxiety. But I suggested that she try to master The Crucial 5s instead. So, I asked her to write down for me how she felt prior to giving a speech. Just like the exercise you just completed. (I *hope* you completed it!) I also asked her to rate her anxiety during a speech. Not surprisingly, this number dropped significantly. That's because deep down, she was in fact ready and a very effective communicator. She was just telling herself all the wrong things prior to giving her presentation. In addition to being the MC, she had to introduce both the president of the network and the senior management team. She was so worried about doing a bad job and *losing* her job that she created her own anxiety!

In a way, her anxiety was certainly understandable, but it would have to be conquered the same way a professional quarterback must conquer his anxiety prior to taking the field during the Super Bowl. Just like that quarterback, she was prepared for the game. We had trained together for weeks leading up to her speech. She had practiced daily and had done her visualization exercises from Principle 3. But right before she took the stage—at the point in which success becomes a mental game—she was stacking the deck against herself by creating unrealistic scenarios and convincing herself that if she made a mistake, she would never recover. In her mind, this unrealistic scenario was the direct cause of her anxiety.

I had Sharon write a very personal affirmation. It read: *I am prepared. Richard and I have practiced for weeks now, and I know this material inside and out. I have been chosen for this assignment because others recognize my skill and my abilities. I am talented. I am ready. I am going to do a great job today and be effective. Everyone will see my gifts, and when it is over, I will feel great for having succeeded. I am ready.*

Sharon read this affirmation several times a day— as soon as she woke up, in the shower, at work, and before she went to bed. She practiced her visualization and added this affirmation into her personal story. Her mind slowly became conditioned to believe what everyone else already knew—that she is a champion. And in the five minutes before she had to stand up in front of international press and the most important people in the television industry, she repeated her affirmations to herself and mentally pictured herself succeeding.

And her mind accepted nothing less than what she told it. Because her anxiety had now gone from a 10 to about a 6, her words came out effortlessly. She smiled and actually enjoyed the moment. In fact, she told me afterward that it was one of the best moments of her entire life. Everyone praised her and told her she made one of the most important days in her network's history a complete success. Most importantly, she enjoyed herself.

When you tell yourself you are a champion, you will act like a champion. Fill your crucial 5's with fuel you need for success.

Remember, public speaking is all about having a conversation. So, start by having a conversation in the privacy of your own home with that investment you're going to make to become a great public speaker— the mirror that you already have in your house. If you make this commitment to yourself and write it down, and if you honor your commitment every day, just a few minutes a day, then you will become a more effective communicator because you'll be doing the one thing that is so essential for every single champion in any field or walk of life—you'll be practicing.

PRINCIPLE 5
DESCRIPTION

Make It Personal and Become a Storyteller

For the end of speech is not ostentation,
but to be understood.

—**William Penn**

DESCRIPTION

Steve didn't have a lot going for him. The biological son of a young, unwed student, Steve was adopted by working-class parents, neither of whom had graduated from college and one of whom hadn't even graduated from high school. Perhaps it came as no surprise, then, that Steve dropped out of college after only six months.

With no clear career vision, over the next year and a half, Steve took a course here and there, struggled to buy food, and lived in various friends' dorm rooms. A tough time, no doubt, but today, Steve will say that dropping out of school was one of the best things he ever did. In fact, he credits his decision to drop out with opening the door for him to pursue his real interests. And pursue them he did. Any idea who Steve is? Read on.

When Steve was twenty, he and a friend started a business. Within ten years, the business had grown to a multibillion-dollar company with thousands of employees. And then, this company that Steve had founded fired him. A tough time, no doubt, but today, Steve will say that getting fired was the best thing to happen to him. Think you might know who Steve is? Keep reading.

Newly jobless, Steve decided to start from scratch ... again. Over the next five years, he founded two more companies, the first of which was eventually bought by the original company Steve founded, and the second of which went on to become the most successful business in its industry. Have you guessed yet?

If you said Steve Jobs, founder of Apple, NeXT, and Pixar, you're right. Like all of us, Steve faced setbacks that, at the time, seemed to be insurmountable. But instead of raising the white flag of surrender, he pressed on and turned his failures into successes.

What's the moral of the story? It can be summed up in Winston Churchill's famous words, "Never give up!"

Beyond the moral, though, I'd wager Steve's story caught your attention and made you want to keep reading, right? The reason is that we all love a story. Stories draw us in, capture our imaginations, and tempt our need to know the ending.

And this proves Principle 5: To be an effective public speaker, make it personal and become a storyteller.

Let's say I'm preparing to give a motivational speech on entrepreneurship. As an example of success, I decide to tell the story of Federal Express. I could give the straightforward historical account of how the Federal Express Corporation was founded in the early 1970s, tell how it was first listed on the New York Stock Exchange in 1978, and give a detailed report of revenue growth over the years.

Yes, I could tell the story this way. But chances are, if I did, my audience would be asleep—or wishing they were—within five minutes. Why? Because people don't care about facts as much as they care about feelings. Let me repeat that: *People don't care about facts as much as they care about feelings.*

This doesn't mean that every speech will—or should for that matter—involve great emotional displays. But every speech, regardless of the occasion, should draw the audience members in and let them *experience* what the speaker is saying.

With this in mind, let's return to my Federal Express speech. How can I bring the timeline to life? Here is one way:

It was the mid 1960s. The conflict in Vietnam was intensifying; IBM had begun distributing business computers, and Frederick Smith was a student at Yale University. With vision ahead of his time, Smith knew that computerization was going to change the face of large-scale distribution, and he wrote a paper about this very thing. Unfortunately, Smith's professor was not quite as forward thinking as Smith and gave the paper a less than stellar grade. Smith could have taken his professor's verdict as truth and shelved the whole idea of computerized distribution. Instead, he took his idea and went on to found Federal Express.

Isn't that much more interesting than "In 1971…In 1978 …" and so on? Of course it is, and the reason is that it relates not only data but also a story of personal struggle and triumph.

Now, think back for a moment to any memorable speech that you've heard. Perhaps it was a graduation address, or a religious message, or a corporate speech—any speech that has stayed in your memory. By any chance did the speaker tell a story? Chances are that he or she did, and that it is the story that you are remembering.

Whatever your opinion is concerning who can or cannot be a "good" public speaker, all of us have it within us to be great storytellers. And stories are critical to human connection.

Consider another example from the world of entertainment. Your favorite movies, plays, or songs are all stories about something. Some of my favorite movies involve a hero going on a journey of discovery and becoming a better person through it. Others are great love stories in which a man and a woman struggle in a relationship, but then end up living "happily ever after." Whatever the plot, the movie or play is a story about something.

On the flip side, think of some films that may have done poorly at the box office. Perhaps they were major action pictures or had majestic cinematography. Regardless of the production talent, chances are these films lacked a depth in their stories (or in the actors' abilities to convey these stories). Sure, they may have experienced initial success, but chances are it was short lived, and these films tend to be ones that are not long remembered.

We've established, then, that storytelling is a critical component of effective speaking, but what exactly does it mean to become a storyteller?

Let me give you an example from one of my own clients at RZC Impact. We'll call her Cynthia.

Cynthia had spent her life in corporate America, having achieved success after overcoming some significant odds. Now, she was ready to embark on a second chapter in her life. Her dream was to start her own company through which she would advise and coach individuals on how they could become successful entrepreneurs. Cynthia came to me because she wanted to polish her speaking and presentation skills in order to put her best foot forward in her new venture.

Like most of us, Cynthia did not lack a story to tell. She had a great one, in fact! It was compelling, relatable, and inspirational. But even though she had all of the right components, she didn't know how to *organize* these components into a cohesive story. And the key to doing this is making it personal.

For example, all of us can tell how a server spilled food on the person at a table next to us in a restaurant, or share what a wonderful time we had on vacation, or give the details of a fantastic concert we attended. But when it comes to giving speeches, we're suddenly at a loss for words. So, instead of putting our whole selves into our speech, we rely on PowerPoint presentations, charts, and facts and figures guaranteed to put even the most interested audience quickly to sleep. Don't misunderstand me. Visual aids have their place, but when we use them as a shield instead of as a supplement, both our audience and our message suffer.

People don't want to be inundated with data. What they really want is to hear something interesting, something that will help them grow while capturing their attention, something that they can take away with them.

So, let's give them what they want.

Cynthia's Story

Let's return to Cynthia. She came into my office already having a story to tell. But when I asked her to tell it and she began to speak, she simply wasn't able to pull it all together. So I gave her a simple exercise. I had her purchase a pack of 3" x 5" index cards and fill them with notes on the following memorable moments in her life:

- The day she decided she wanted to work in corporate America
- Her first day on the job
- The toughest day she ever had at work
- How she felt on that day

Once we had these bases covered, I decided to dig a bit deeper with Cynthia. Taking a few more index cards, I asked her to jot down some additional thoughts and recollections:

- What did her parents and family think of her entering corporate America?
- Had she followed her family's wishes? Or had they wanted something else for her life?
- Looking back, what was she most proud of and why?

Notice that as we progressed further into the exercise, the theme of the cards began moving from facts to feelings, from "I started work on this date" to "This is how I felt when I accomplished such and such."

Once Cynthia had filled up several cards, I had her stand in front of a mirror and read through the cards—not in any formal manner, but rather just read through them chronologically. As she did, she began to tell the story of her life, the story of a woman who had started out on a journey with certain goals in mind, but not knowing exactly where the path would take her. The story of making the decision to work in corporate America, of what she experienced when she arrived, of the obstacles she faced and overcame, and of working her way up the corporate ladder. Beyond simply relating facts, Cynthia shared her first big challenge, her first failure, and her first realization that things were not as easy as she had imagined they would be.

By the time Cynthia finished, she had shared with me, her "audience," how she had set a goal and achieved it and, ultimately, what that could mean for everyone else.

Of course, not everyone will have a story like Cynthia's. Perhaps your story has nothing to do with working in corporate America or even with career matters at all. Maybe your story is about how you faced and overcame an illness, how you went back to school later in life, or how you planned a surprise birthday party for your significant other.

Whatever the topic—whether a major life decision or an everyday occurrence—you have a story to tell, and it's one that you can tell in a way that no one else can.

How Many Stories Does Your Story Have?

Stories come in all shapes, sizes, and depths. For example, I could tell how my choice of a college affected my future career path, or I could tell you about what I ate for breakfast this morning. Some stories we tell because they have great moral or inspirational value, and other stories we tell in order to break the ice and establish a rapport with our audience. Whatever the story—whether inspirational, anecdotal, or humorous—it can help make your speech powerful, memorable, and, most importantly, effective.

But how do you know where and how a particular story should fit into your speech? I like to use a technique I call "The Stories of A Story." Picture a building—any type of building. What do you see? Perhaps a towering skyscraper against a city skyline? Or a country cottage surrounded by a garden? Maybe you're picturing a meticulously landscaped office building with spotless, reflecting windows. Whatever type of building you've imagined, it has a certain number of floors—or stories—to it. And just as the structure as a whole has a main purpose—be it professional space, public space, or living space—so each story in the building has a purpose.

A speech is exactly like a building.

Every speech has a purpose, or overarching "story"—be it training, inspiration, persuasion, or entertainment. This is the speech "building." Within that building, the parts of the speech are the floors, or "stories." Each story has a purpose and contributes to the overall purpose of the speech.

For example, if I am giving a speech about professional networking, this theme will be the speech "building." In order to construct a strong building, I will need to include several "stories." The number of stories depends on the scope of the speech. For a speech on networking, my stories may look something like this:

- Local chambers of commerce
- Industry associations
- Online networking tools
- Family and friends

• Current and past colleagues

As I talk about each one of these topics and share experiences related to each, I will be building a structure that is my overall message. This is important to remember when preparing your storytelling notes for a speech, as we will do in the section below.

From Theory to Practice: Making it Work

Are you ready to dig in and put the principles of effective storytelling into practice? Here is your assignment. For practice purposes, let's make your current job or career the topic of this exercise.

1. Buy a set of 3" x 5" or 5" x 8" index cards.
2. On these cards, write down the facts about the memorable moments related to this topic. Use a separate card for each moment. Topics your cards may include are:
    a. The day you decided to take your job or start your business
    b. Your first day at work
    c. Your toughest day at work
3. Now, go back through these cards and fill in the feelings surrounding the facts.
    d. What made you decide to take the job? Launch out on your own? Was it a difficult decision?
    e. What did others think about your choice? Did their opinions sway you? If so, how? If not, why not?
    f. How did you feel your first day on the job? Excited? Nervous? Confident? Unsure?

g.   What happened to make your toughest day tough?
How did you react to the circumstances? How did
you feel? What did you do to handle it?

As you go through this exercise, write down whatever
comes to mind, regardless of how insignificant it may seem.
Although it may not be the main point of your speech, it may
turn out to be an important building block that makes your
speech effective. Remember, no thought is too insignificant
at this initial stage. You can always go through and edit
later. So, write down everything: failures, successes, great
moments you wish could happen again, moments you wish
never happened, and people you met along the way. As one
memory jogs another, put it on the appropriate card.

Once you've done this, take a moment to organize
your cards. All great stories have three things in common:
a beginning, a middle, and an end. Capturing and respecting this structure is essential to effective communication
because audiences are trained by experience to listen to the
beginning, identify when the speaker is in the middle, or
"heart," of the talk, and recognize when the speech is ending. As you speak, your job is to take your listeners on your
journey with you—bring them with you as you take your
new job, start your new business, and face the struggles that
are an inevitable part of any new venture.

With this in mind, once you have your cards written out,
arrange them in chronological order and number them.
(Numbering is a very important habit to get into. In the
event you are giving a speech and you drop your cards or
they fall off the podium, for example, numbering ensures you

will be able quickly and easily to put them back in order and continue with your talk.)

Now, take your ordered and numbered cards and stand in front of a mirror in your home or office. Preferably, it should be a full-length mirror, but any wall mirror will do. Start with card number 1, and begin to tell your story. Don't worry at this point about wording or body language. Simply go through the cards and relate the facts and feelings about the points you wrote down. Soon, you'll notice that your story is taking shape. You're telling about a memorable event in your life, and then you're telling *why* it was memorable and *how* it affected you. This is what a great story is—not only the "what" but also the "why" and the "how." People are much more interested in the motivations behind human actions and reactions than they are in the actions and reactions themselves. Feelings put facts in context.

As you practice telling your story, you will probably think of additional points. Pause to jot them down as well. Each memory you add about how you acted, thought, or felt makes the story more personal and, hence, makes your speech more effective.

This practice technique applies regardless of the type of speech you're giving—whether a wedding toast in front of family and friends or a business address to a roomful of company executives. The reason is that the principles of human nature are constant across the board. All of us share the common traits of struggle, persistence, perseverance, accomplishment, failures, success, heartbreak, love, and death. These are the very things that make us human and bond us together, and the more we can talk about them as speakers—in any and every setting—the more people are going to listen to what we have to say and appreciate and enjoy our speech.

So, even if you're talking about your company's financial forecast for the year, you can still frame it in such a way that you are inspiring your team to great achievement and creating a goal that you and they can accomplish together.

Remember what we talked about in Principle 1? *You already have everything you need to become an effective public speaker.* It's already within you. Now, we just have to get it out.

So, don't think about your life or your career or whatever your message may be simply in terms of a timeline. Think of it as a story.

Remember Cynthia, who started out not knowing how to tell the story of her life? She now speaks to groups and shares with them her story—the story of a young woman who overcame obstacles, including opposition from family and friends, to take a job in corporate America with a start-up company that was failing and, realistically speaking, had no prospects for success. Cynthia tells how she had a vision and a goal in her mind of one day becoming the executive of that company. She shares how that company grew to become one of the most successful telecommunications companies in American history and how she did, indeed, earn the title of Madame Executive.

Cynthia's story is a great story because it is filled with triumphs, setbacks, perseverance, and victory.

You have a great story to tell, too. And you, too, *can* tell it effectively if you simply practice the principle of making it personal.

PRINCIPLE
INSPIRATION 6

Speak to Serve

" *As long as there are human rights to be defended, as long as there are great interests to be guarded, as long as the welfare of nations is a matter for discussion, so long will public speaking have its place.* **"**

—William Jennings Bryan

INSPIRATION

When you're up on stage or in front of the company's board of directors giving a speech, it's very easy to get caught up in the idea that you are the most important person in the room. Well, I have some news for you. You're not—not even close. The most important "person" in the room is always going to be the audience, and this rule holds true whether you are a professional public speaker, vice president of your company, or president of the United States. The most important people are always the people who are listening to the speech, not the person doing the talking, and this is where Principle 6—Speak to Serve—comes into play.

This principle is crucial in making an invaluable human connection with an audience and ensuring that the audience members feel you have their best interests at heart. It's about understanding the audience and understanding your role as a speaker.

The most effective communicators are the ones who not only make us feel comfortable and relaxed but also have a purpose in what they're trying to say—and when we listen to them, we understand our personal stake in the subject. Good speakers relate to us, and we feel a connection. And this is true regardless of the topic of the speech.

Speaking to serve is a critical tool to use when you talk about your business, your company, or yourself, and it is a tool that can change everything you've ever thought about public speaking.

Now, I know that we all think that our goal as public speakers is to get up and be engaging and dynamic, and all that may be true, but the most important goal we should have is to serve our audience members either by talking about something that interests them or by making an otherwise uninteresting topic interesting. This is what people really want.

When you think about it, the objective of most speeches is not to benefit the speaker but to benefit the audience, and in all likelihood, the purpose of your presentation is, in some way, to help your audience through teaching, motivation, entertainment, or education. While the audience's focus may be on you, you're not the most important party in the room—your audience is. Your ultimate focus should be helping the audience. In practical terms, this means that in all your preparation and presentation, I want you consistently to think about how you can help your audience members achieve their goals.

When you do this, your role as a speaker becomes a role of service to the needs of the audience, and this is a great way to make a human connection. If you can remember this one fact, then public speaking becomes less an act of fear and more an opportunity to serve others.

Now, how do you put this into action in your own life?

Most people simply talk about what it is they do in a matter-of-fact way without explaining what is "in it" for the audience. And it's not just a matter of describing a special product that can save your listeners money or a service you can provide to coach their business. It's more than that. It's about connecting to your audience members on a far deeper level because you start with their interests in mind.

Gary's Story

Gary is one of the most talented entrepreneurs I have ever had the pleasure to work with. He understands the value of continuous growth and self-improvement as it relates not only to his business but also to his personal life. He is a man who is always striving to improve his life and the lives of his customers. While he didn't always realize it, he provided a service so beneficial that he actually helped businesses succeed, be more productive, and dramatically improve employee morale. In fact, I will tell you that Gary has directly helped the economy because he has helped small and even large businesses comfortably deal with the day-to-day challenges of running their operations. His customers are happy and productive, and they love coming to work every day.

What does Gary do? you ask. *What does this man sell that has such a direct effect on people's personal well-being and economic growth?*

Gary sells office furniture.

That's right. But Gary doesn't just sell office furniture; he designs productivity. When he first contacted me, however, he didn't know his real occupation just yet. He thought (perhaps like you did when you saw what he does) that he only sells furniture.

Gary called me and told me he had won the opportunity to give a five-minute speech before hundreds of business owners. The event was only a few weeks away, and he was nervous. He wasn't an experienced speaker, but he recognized that this was a tremendous opportunity for him to reach hundreds of new customers without having to spend a penny in advertising.

I told him to prepare a five-minute outline of what he wanted to discuss. We set up a meeting, and I came to his office building, which also serves as his warehouse. I was impressed. Gary's company is one of the largest supply companies on the eastern seaboard, and he serves clients all over the country.

Gary began with the line, "My ideal customer is the customer who is in the market for new office furniture and equipment."

With that line, he was right away probably turning off 75 percent of the audience and greatly limiting his potential. Perhaps everyone in the room was in the market for new furniture and equipment; they just didn't know it yet.

Then, like most speakers, Gary began to explain in a matter-of-fact way what his company does.

"We sell office furniture and equipment such as desks, chairs, lighting, and just about every other office furnishing you can think of."

Then, he concluded with a direct appeal to the audience.

"So, if you are ever in the market, feel free to come by our showroom or give us a call and check us out."

Okay, pretty standard and incredibly boring. But I didn't say that.

Then Gary looked at me and said, "That's all I have so far." It was then that I realized why Gary needed me to help his business grow, and it was also then that I realized I should have charged him more!

"Let's take a walk around your showroom," I said to Gary.

Gary took me inside his mammoth facility, and I was truly impressed. The variety of offerings he had would satisfy just about any business. There was no end to the possibilities.

"Gary," I began, "tell me about the process. Pretend I'm someone who might want new furniture. How do we begin?"

"First, we come to your office and look at your space," he answered.

Already, I realized this was something that set Gary apart from his competitors and provided a valuable service. He then went on to explain to me that for every work space, his company would analyze how much light each individual area was getting, identify the best place to put the power cords, and evaluate the best style of furniture for the confines of the office. Gary didn't just sell office furniture; he carefully designed individual spaces to maximize productivity and effectiveness.

I helped Gary realize that his business wasn't really furniture. Technically, that is the means by which he delivered his business, but his business was actually increasing productivity and employee morale. Anyone who is a manager understands how important both are to the bottom line. How did Gary achieve this? His team did a custom analysis of each space to determine all of the factors that contribute to productivity, and then they designed an office based upon the individual needs of the client.

This is the essence of serving the client. Now, how do we translate that into serving the audience?

At the core of the Speak to Serve principle is an understanding that there is a bond between the speaker and the audience. Audiences want you to succeed. They want to feel good for having listened to your remarks. Audiences don't go into a speech hoping that you will fail, hoping that you will bore them to death, hoping that you will say essentially the same things everyone else says. Audiences are secretly rooting for you. They would love nothing more than for a speaker to get up to the podium and hit the ball out of the park. So Speak to Serve, and begin with the audience members in mind. Serve them by keeping the speech interesting and making them understand their stake in it and they will root for you even more!

For Gary, his speech now began with a question. He would ask his listeners to close their eyes and picture their work space. He asked them if they were comfortable, if they had enough room on their desk, and if they had enough light to see clearly or if they were constantly squinting. "Keep your eyes closed," he said, "and feel yourself sitting in your chair. Is it comfortable, or does your back hurt? Are you straining to reach the keyboard? Okay, open your eyes.

"My name is Gary and my company provides increased productivity and enhanced employee morale. We come to your space and create a custom-tailored solution based on your individual needs. Does anyone in the room feel this is something that would interest them?"

Of course just about everyone in the audience felt this was something that would interest him or her, and at the conclusion of the speech, people were practically jumping over themselves to ask Gary to visit their office and do a free consultation. As an added bonus, Gary ended his speech with five tips for reducing carpal tunnel syndrome at the office and handed everyone a little guide he had compiled on proper office chair alignment.

The difference between this type of presentation and the typical presentation—in which someone walks in and simply explains what his or her business does, then expects you to buy something when you have absolutely no idea how it benefits you—is like the difference between night and day. Gary served his audience in the following ways:

- He made the speech interesting. Instead of just stating what his business does, he made it interactive and involved his listeners.
- He made the speech relevant. Who doesn't sit in a chair during the workday? And how many times do we wish that our keyboard were bigger, that the artificial lighting would stop giving us headaches, and that the chair were just a little more comfortable?
- He empathized with the audience members by assuring them he understood their struggle to have a productive and energizing work space.
- He left the audience members both with free tips that would provide immediate results and with a way to remember him when they left the speech, returned to their offices, and sat in their chairs.
- He found a way to make his speech *about* the audience rather than just about him.

All in all, Gary did an excellent job of speaking to serve.

Just last week I had the opportunity to hear Gary speak again, this time after he was a fully credited graduate of the 7 Principles of Public Speaking. I was extremely impressed by his progress. Gary took hold of the microphone and immediately told the audience a story that involved them in the process and clearly showed them their stake in the process. There was no question that he understood this principle when he pulled out an ergonomic office chair and asked the audience to imagine themselves sitting in the chair enjoying the benefits this beautiful black leather chair with lumbar support could provide. Then he asked the audience to guess how much his competitor sold it for, which was over a hundred dollars more expensive than his price, and gave the chair away to the person who came closest to guessing correctly. Talk about Speak to Serve! He clearly showed his audience how his business could benefit them, he involved the audience, and he did it all in only four minutes as opposed to the five minutes he was allotted.

Gary won over the crowd that morning, especially the woman who won the chair! He is literally transformed as a speaker, and the same can happen to you as we complete this journey together. Interestingly, the speaker who spoke immediately following Gary, spoke for three minutes longer than his allotted time, did not tell a single story, and at no point during the speech, connected with his audience. At the end of the speech, Gary handed him his used copy of my guide to the 7 Principles of Public Speaking. I considered this a tremendous compliment.

Now you don't necessarily have to give away free chairs, but you do have to clearly understand what value you really provide to your audience. How can you serve your audience the next time you give a speech?

In the space below, write down three products or services that either you or your company provides to your consumer base:

1. _____
2. _____
3. _____

Now, for each of these, think about ways that they enriched the lives of your customers or your family members or the people in your community—literally, any people with whom you come in contact.

For example, if your business is the mortgage business and your job is to get up at community business meetings and talk about your company and your products and services, is there a new loan product specifically designed for members of this community? Is there a way they can pay down their mortgages sooner? Or perhaps your company does work to provide programs designed to help low-income individuals or families. The key is to relate your business or service to the needs of your audience members. Instead of just talking about your company or your product, talk about how it benefits your audience.

If you're in the insurance industry, perhaps you can talk about a great program that can protect people if, God forbid, they should get a certain illness or have their house flooded. Consider leaving your audience with a takeaway that provides instructions on how to prepare for an emergency or tips on how to reduce accidents. The point is to always think about how what you do can benefit your audience.

I have a client who started a great business in which he actually advises corporations on how to spend their philanthropic funds. He gets up in front of executives and talks to them about how they can use their money to improve the lives of other people. When he had the opportunity to give a speech to a local organization, instead of just stating what he did, he brought in people whose lives had been changed by the philanthropic work of one of his clients. Then he provided each member of the audience with a fact sheet designed to help him or her understand the tax benefits of contributing to organizations. In brief, he gave his audience a one-two punch by showing both the humanitarian and the economic benefits of philanthropy. And most important of all, he did it an interesting manner.

Maybe you're a landscaper and you want to talk about how your landscaping business has helped beautify streets that once were not very beautiful. This is an important community contribution, and your audience will appreciate that. If this is you, you might drive home your point by providing your audience members with ideas on how they can beautify their own home or neighborhood streets. Always consider, "How can this benefit someone else?"

If you approach your speech with this in mind, your audience will remember you long after you've left the podium.

I know some people who own a chocolate gift shop. They spent some time at a breakfast recently talking about their wide selection of dark chocolate products and the medical evidence that shows that dark chocolate can help prevent heart attacks. And of course, as a takeaway, everyone received a piece of their delicious chocolate as well as a fact sheet on the benefits of antioxidants in products such as, you guessed it, chocolate.

The Speaker Challenge

Your challenge as a speaker is to figure out listeners' needs and then show how your product or service fills those needs.

If you're in the company boardroom and you are going to talk about your company's sales forecast, serve your audience members by relaying to them how you're going to achieve your sales goals based on your skills and the skills of your team. For example, "We project that we're going to have a 10 percent increase this year, and the way we're going to do this is to pull in these five people. Here are their talents. Here's how we're going to make this happen." Always ask yourself, "How can I serve my listeners? How can I make this clear to them? How can I show them what's at stake for them? How can I show them how I can make their life, company, product, or service better?" If you do this, then you will force yourself to come up with more details and examples to make your speech engaging. It takes a little work, and it's not always easy to do. But as we as champions know, the best things in life are not always easy, but they are usually the most rewarding.

When I talk about the fact that I'm a communications coach, I say that I help people overcome their fear and anxiety so they can become more effective communicators and more productive in life and, as a result, have a richer life because they don't have to be afraid anymore of going to family weddings and communions just because they might have to give a toast. It's all about understanding that what people are really asking speakers is, "What's my stake in this process? What can you do for me?" And no one out there has a job that's so boring that it doesn't in some way benefit others.

Remember what I said in Principle 1: You already have everything you need to become an effective communicator. You just have to get it out. Remember Cynthia from Principle 5? She had years and years of wisdom and inspiration to give to people who wanted to take the risk of starting their own business and become entrepreneurs, but it wasn't until we broke down her story using the index card method and she finally saw what she had learned and overcome in life that she was able to get up on stage and talk about her experiences, inspiring others in the process! This is exactly what I mean by "Speak to Serve."

Think about how you, your product, your service, or your company can help other people. Make it real. Make it relevant. Search for the good you do and, if nothing else, remember that what people always want to know is how you are really just like them.

The Client Pitch

Speak to Serve is incredibly effective when making a one-on-one client pitch, and it will have dramatic results when you are trying to close a sale, land a new client, or win new business.

The Radio Station

Recently I did a communication training seminar for the sales force of a major radio corporation. Their territory included three states and served many different types of businesses, all of which had the goal of improving their bottom line. The sales personnel did not have an easy job, however, as they often had to persuade businesses of their need to advertise on the radio when that need was not always apparent. In addition, the sales force had to convince existing customers to come back and advertise again.

After leading the organization in a communications overview, I spent one-on-one time with each sales professional working on his "pitch." Pitch U is a program that I've taught at my company, RZC Impact, with great success. The principle of Speak to Serve is the foundation of this program's effectiveness.

I worked with each member of the team by doing a mock pitch, in which I played the role of the potential customer. The team member then had to "pitch" me about advertising on the radio. A few of the participants were naturals, and they immediately grasped the concept of Speak to Serve and made their pitches all about me. Several others, however, immediately began the pitch by stating what they do and what they "could do for me." To me, this always sounds manipulative, because I know that what you can do for me is usually persuade me to spend money, and that's probably not what I want. So, I asked each participant to answer the following questions about the company and their role:

- Write down the ways in which the company benefits the client.
- Write down the ways in which your role benefits the client.
- Write down the ways in which you help or have helped your clients.

Then I challenged each team member to answer the following questions about their prospect:

- What does this company/person do for a living?
- How successful are they at the present time and how successful have they been in the past?
- Who is their target audience?
- What should be their "message" to reach and connect with that audience?
- What would be a unique way for them to serve that audience?

Stop for a moment and reread that last statement. How many salespeople just go to meet with someone and explain all the great benefits of their product or service, yet fail to articulate how their prospect's situation would improve by using that product or service?

When you go into a pitch, clearly show your prospect a) the benefit of your product or service, b) your past successes helping others, and c) how you can serve your prospect. Do your homework and make your pitch specific to the needs of the potential client.

One of the team members, Tom, was challenged to convince a start-up business, a winery, to advertise on the radio. He did his homework and knew the winery inside and out. The owner was a true visionary who believed he was making an invaluable contribution to tourism in his area. The clientele consisted of wine lovers and also people who just enjoyed spending a nice day outside sipping homemade wine in an Italian farmhouse setting. Tom answered the speaker challenge questions right away and found an example of another start-up that someone on his team helped in the past through guiding it in hosting an event designed to bring customers to the business as opposed to relying on advertising alone. Tom also found a way to create a proposal for the client that showed how he could positively help them achieve similar growth and do so while also serving the audience.

The solution was to hold an open house at the winery and to advertise the event on the radio. This was a cost-effective way for the start-up entrepreneur to attract new customers to his business. The client was able to serve his customers by bringing them into his facility for a free night at the vineyard, and Tom was able to serve his client by proactively suggesting a solution that enabled him to attract customers and show them his business.

Here was the message: *Have you ever dreamed of spending time in California wine county or touring the vineyards of Tuscany, but you can't travel too far from home? Welcome to Cara Winery, a taste of Tuscany in our own backyard. Join us for the grand opening celebration.*

In all your preparation and presentation, constantly think of how you can help your audience members achieve their goals, whether it's through providing their children with the means to go through college, offering inspiration to help others overcome the odds, showing fresh ways to help the company soar to new profits and new heights, or just giving away dark chocolate to help people get through their cravings and possibly prevent heart disease.

In doing this, you as a speaker assume a role of service to your audience. When this happens, public speaking becomes less an act of fear and more an opportunity to serve others. Most important, your speeches will be more interesting and your audience will remember you for a long time to come.

Key points:
- Always remember the speech isn't about you; it's about your audience.
- Serve your audience by making the speech interesting.
- Understand what service your business truly provides, not just what products you sell.
- Discover a link between what you provide and what your listeners want in their daily lives.
- Never state what it is you do as matter of fact; rather, explain it in a way that shows the audience members how they will benefit from what you do.
- Consider the use of takeaways that provide a service and ensure you will be remembered long after your speech concludes.
- Make sure the takeaways have all your pertinent contact information, are useful to your audience, and tie into your speech in some fashion.

How to Use Public Speaking to Promote Your Business

Public speaking is an integral part of every successful business. That's right, whether you're in sales or accounting, public speaking can help you promote your business.

One of my clients is a labor attorney who struggled for clients. He found that traditional advertising simply wasn't working and was becoming too expensive. His firm periodically sent out newsletters about the cases in which he was involved, but he had a sense very few people were actually taking time out of their day to read the newsletters and understand the benefits his services could provide to them.

When he called me for advice, I suggested he hold a seminar on labor issues people face on a daily basis. I recommended he talk about common issues that small business owners would benefit from understanding, such as payroll tax, equal opportunity laws, and immigration issues.

He held the seminar and invited dozens of small business owners from the community to attend free of charge. A few weeks went by, and he e-mailed me to let me know that he had picked up several clients as a result of holding the seminar. The event was a success.

And the event involved public speaking.

Selecting Your Topic

Great speeches always serve a purpose, and your business services, combined with a compelling presentation, will not only help you prosper but also help the community. This is the essence of Speak to Serve.

If you are a chiropractor, perhaps holding a free talk at a local health club or library on ways to prevent a pulled back would be an ideal way to promote your business and provide a valuable and needed public service.

If you are a landscaper, how about a free presentation on ways to beautify your lawn? Include tips on growing an herb garden, and invite a local florist and a chef to co-sponsor the event. They will, no doubt, appreciate the exposure, and your business will grow.

If you are a Wall Street investor with a six-figure income and a great job at a hedge fund, consider holding an event on investing. Even if you may not have a need to start your own business now, you may find it draws more clients to the firm.

Determining the Need You Can Fill

The question is not whether a need exists; it is *what* need exists that your business can meet. Here are a few questions to ask yourself. Answer these questions and you will soon see "the need" emerging!

What products or services does my company offer?

To whom does it offer them? Who/What/Where is my market? Examples: seniors, women, small business owners, homeowners, students, or health care consumers. The list is endless.

What motivates people to use the products and services my business offers?

How can people truly benefit from what I do?

> How would people's lives improve if they learned from
> the advice I had to offer?
>
> How do I reach people?

The last question is always the trickiest one, but rest assured, if you offer a message that truly fills a need, people will come to hear you. If you speak it, they will come.

When holding an event, offer your audience some light refreshments: coffee, cookies, other snacks. There is no need to go overboard and cater a full buffet, but a little nourishment goes a long way.

Early in my career, before I started coaching *Fortune* 500 executives, I was struggling to find clients outside the political arena. I wanted very much to reach out to the small business community as my first step. I knew that if I could demonstrate the benefits of public speaking and media training to small business owners, they would want to hire me to help them better communicate and grow their business.

I contacted the president of the local chamber of commerce and offered to host a complimentary seminar on public speaking. As it turned out, the chamber regularly hosted a free monthly business breakfast, and the attendance averaged more than two hundred small business leaders. For breakfast!

When I told the chamber leader that I would do the event and would not charge, she was very excited to offer her membership such a great opportunity for their development. She promoted the event heavily, sending out a newsletter about my company, my background, and the program. This was a tremendous benefit for me because my company was reaching hundreds of prominent business leaders—and potential clients—and I didn't have to pay a dime for the exposure.

About fifty small business leaders attended the event and I did my best to present a thorough and well-organized presentation. I made up color public speaking workbooks, called on members from the audience, and involved the local business community in my efforts.

The results were great. I gained a built-in list of potential clients, and word quickly spread about my services and how they could benefit small business owners. Soon, people who had to give speeches called on me for training. An added benefit was that several of the members in attendance had contacts at larger businesses and corporations in the area. The members reached out to these other leaders on my behalf, and soon I had the opportunity to meet executives from prominent corporations who were looking for training for their entire sales teams. This led to working with the senior management team at one corporation, and soon after, a prominent CEO at another. Word travels fast! And all this came from giving a free seminar on the benefits of effective communication.

Imagine what this same idea can do for your business. The key is to personalize the program for the audience at hand.

BONUS PRINCIPLE: STAYING ON MESSAGE

BONUS PRINCIPLE: STAYING ON MESSAGE

When you watch major candidates for political office on television, it is easy to become enamored of their ability to articulate so effortlessly. We are often impressed with their talent for speaking candidly in front of large groups, handling tough questions, and participating in debates with the nation's leading journalists. Would it surprise you to know that these candidates spend hours doing debate prep, speech prep, and media prep? The fact that major league players all undergo significant training shows us just how challenging effective communication can be without the right tools. But the good news for all of us is that it also shows that if they can do it, so can we.

I have helped train several candidates for political office over the years, and one approach I often take is that of playing the role of either a reporter or an opponent. And I can attest to the fact that the axiom "stay on message" is a phrase by which campaigns and candidates live and die. Politicians and the press play a delicate chess game with each other. The press tries very hard to make the politician answer something he or she doesn't want to answer. The politician tries at all times to answer the question in a way that will ensure his or her message gets out loud and clear, no matter what.

Staying on message is about controlling the context of the message and not allowing other people or circumstances to detract from or in any way change what you want to say.

In the 1992 race for the White House, the message, as you may remember, was "It's the economy, stupid." And this message was preached time and again by James Carville.

In 2004, the message for both candidates was keeping America safe.

Many political pundits blame Rudy Giuliani's failure to gain the Republican presidential nomination in 2008 on the fact that he was "off-message" in his campaign and spent a significant amount of time talking about terrorism when the country was once again concerned with the economy.

Similarly, analysts will point to Barack Obama's success in the primary election as the result of his staying on message about change.

In politics, the message can change almost hourly, and politicians and their highly paid operatives work diligently to keep the candidates on their message. Most campaigns have a "message of the week" or "message of the day." For an entire week or day, they may talk about nothing but the environment or taxes or health care, for example. But what does this mean for us? How do we learn to stay on message and not get pulled in different directions? Staying on message is a very important part of public speaking and of effective communication in general, and it is a critical lesson to master.

Staying on message is about gaining control over how the audience perceives you and what you are discussing. We have discussed how easily an audience can become distracted, but it is even easier for a speaker to become distracted by a tough question or a question that seems to come from left field and throws the speaker for a loop.

First and foremost, you have to know what your message is. What are you trying to get across? Discovering the central theme of your message is the first step in this process.

If you think back to English class, when you first learned how to construct a thesis, you probably learned the importance of opening a term paper with a few lines that serve as the thesis, or main point, you are going to prove. As speakers, we should follow this rule as well. Before you speak, go into an interview, or talk to the press, think carefully about the central point you are going to prove. This is the message that you need to convey early on in your interview or speech.

The message is your key point, and everything that follows is used to prove that point. The message should be one line. The one line that is going to be the basis for your entire speech. Everything else follows after this one line.

Message examples:
- *I am the best person for this job.*
- *Our firm is best equipped for this project.*
- *I will fix our broken economy.*
- *Nantucket is the best place to visit over the summer.*
- *The_____ Party won't do anything to control rising gas prices.*

- *Invest your money with our firm and watch with confidence as it grows.*
- *Faith is the most precious gift.*
- *Perseverance is the key ingredient to success.*
- *List your home with us and watch it sell!*
- *Our company is dedicated to the safety of our consumers.*
- *We take full responsibility for this and pledge to immediately address the problem.*

Everything that follows from this point forward will ultimately be used to prove your main point. But before you can prove your point, you must first prove your credibility before your audience. Only if you do this successfully will your audience—or the press—believe that you have the expertise to know what you are talking about.

The Credibility Connection

If a candidate for the presidency who was fired from every job he ever held in his entire life gave a major address on the economy, you would probably dismiss him outright as having no credibility on the subject. That is, unless you didn't know that he was fired from every job he ever held and he articulated his position in a manner that clearly proved he knew what he was talking about, citing extensive research on the subject or stories to prove his point. Similarly, a candidate who is a Nobel Prize–winning economist but fails to let the audience know this and doesn't take the time necessary to build his credibility through examples and research will probably be viewed as underqualified and his message similarly dismissed.

I'm not making this up. We see it all the time.

Audiences have their own ways to determine who and what is credible, and that is why it is important to make a credibility connection with your audience before you try to prove your message.

To gain credibility with an audience, clearly state what gives you the right to speak on your subject. Examples might be:

- Experience in the area
- Educational background
- Awards
- Published articles
- Specific knowledge
- Research
- Past accomplishments
- Detailed plan of action

Principles in Action

John from Genesis Engineering wants everyone to understand that his engineering company can handle the project of building a new bridge between New York and New Jersey. So, the message is, "Our company has the expertise to handle this project, and we should be awarded the contract."

John will use the first few lines of his speech for the introduction, but then he will quickly state his message: "Hi, my name is John, thank you for coming tonight. I'd like to tell you a little about my company, Genesis Engineering, and explain that we are in fact, best suited to be chosen as the company to build the new $2.1 billion bridge."

Now it is time for John to make a credibility connection with his audience. He might use this time to let the audience know he graduated from one of the top engineering universities in America, or he might use an example of other major bridges his company has designed and built. John has to decide how best to use the limited amount of time he has to establish his credibility connection: "I graduated from Engineering University of America." Or "I helped design and build a very successful bridge."

Similarly, there are many ways for us to explain our credibility, but we always want to think about the strongest points that maximize our credibility on the subject. In John's case, his best option would be to explain that he helped build the George Washington Bridge, the Brooklyn Bridge, and the Golden Gate Bridge. This establishes his credibility and reinforces his message.

Once you establish your credibility, it is time to prove your point while staying on message using examples and stories. This is the dangerous sea where speakers often find their ships crashing into the infinite morass of choices. We can speak about so many things, but the less focused our message, the more likely that we will go off course. Consider your message like a laser beam. You want to carefully aim it at your target. Everything that is said must be used to support your message with precision, because if you get off-message, you may find it difficult ever to come back.

Ask yourself:

What examples can I use to support my message?

_____

_____

_____

Is there a story I can tell to support my message or enhance my credibility?

_____

_____

_____

What important facts and figures do I need to convey to support my message?

_____

_____

_____

The rule is simple: If it doesn't support your message, replace it with something that does.

John may think this is an opportune time for him to share a story about his experience working on a tunnel project. It may be tempting for him to tell a funny story about how he had dirt fall on his head during a tunnel inspection, but that doesn't help prove his point: that he and his firm are qualified to build a bridge. He needs to stay on message and tell a story that helps prove the fact that his company is, in fact, best suited to build the new $2.1 billion bridge.

Perhaps John should tell a story about another bridge project he worked on that was able to save the client time and money. By telling the story, John will reassert his credibility while keeping the audience interested. The audience will hear the story and think, "Wow, this guy really knows what he is talking about." As we learned in Principle 5, stories have power. Simply stating experience is not nearly as powerful or effective as telling a story that shows experience.

After John has spent a few minutes building his credibility, he should move on to explain why his company should build this particular bridge. If you are wondering why he shouldn't get to that part sooner, it is because he *must* establish credibility before people will accept what he is saying as fact. If John were simply to start talking about why he could build the bridge without giving the expertise and story that *prove* his thesis, he would not be staying on message. The message is, "We have the expertise." Well, stay on message and prove your claim to us!

After establishing his credibility, John can speak about the specific project at hand, explaining why his firm should get the job because he will save the city or state money while building the safest, most advanced bridge possible. Assuming John follows this method, the audience has already accepted John's credibility and will be receptive to his message.

Now it is time for the closing. At this point, John should rephrase his thesis, "We are best suited for this $2.1 billion bridge project because we will build the safest, most affordable, most advanced bridge possible, and this is evidenced by our twenty-five years of experience and solid credentials." He's restated the thesis, and now he can close his speech.

"I hope you all enjoyed your dinner. Thank you again for coming. Good night."

The net result is that John stayed on message and the audience walked out thinking, *This guy is right, he really is best suited for this project. He really knows what's he's talking about.*

Recently, I conducted a three-day, intensive communications seminar with fourteen senior directors of a large northeastern engineering firm. The goal of the training was to help each director understand how to communicate the firm's message. When I first arrived, I was amazed to see just how off-message the directors were as a group. Each of fourteen directors overseeing a different department within the larger company articulated a different message about the firm and about his or her areas of expertise. Like many growing organizations, this firm suffered from an inability to articulate its growth and define its future goals.

We began the training with an overview of the seven principles by making the principles specific to that company and its unique needs. Each director then worked directly with me one-on-one and gave me his "pitch." We filmed each session, and I reviewed the pitch with each person individually. It is remarkable how quickly people can adopt a new style when they have the opportunity to view their performance on camera. Little habits of posture and speaking styles that we are unaware of come to the forefront and I highly recommend videotaping as a way of analyzing and improving style.

After the one-on-one sessions, I reported back to the firm's president and executive vice president and told them that they, indeed, had a problem. No one in senior management knew the firm's message, and you can imagine that if no one in senior management knew the message, certainly neither did anyone in junior management. So we brought the entire group back into the room and asked the directors a series of questions about the firm so they could work as a group to understand how to construct a message specific and unique to their particular audience. Since the firm handled multi-million-dollar bridge, tunnel, and highway projects and also provided municipal engineering services to small rural communities, providing an overview became increasingly challenging. The firm also had challenges in the sense that it had grown to the point where it was no longer a small firm, but at the same time it wasn't quite a large firm yet. This meant that many of its smaller clients wanted the individual attention only a small firm could provide, so their growing size could be seen as intimidating, while many other prospects were gigantic engineering firms they wanted to partner with, who might view them as too small for their workload.

The firm also had the challenge of geography. Its headquarters are in New Jersey, but it also had offices in New York, Connecticut, Massachusetts, Delaware, Maryland, and Pennsylvania—areas that represented several unique markets with specific and unique needs. Tailoring the message to suit the particular market would be vital.

The following memorandum is one the company's director of corporate communications created based upon the training session. As you follow along, consider how you would answer these questions for your own company. Understanding how you define key areas such as size, success, and vision is essential to success. Consider creating a similar guide for you and your team or reaching out to a communications trainer to conduct an in-house program to facilitate this important discussion. Remember, your team truly is your greatest asset. They represent the company twenty-four hours a day, and whenever they are speaking about the company, publicly or privately, it is essential to ensure they have the right message.

★ ★ ★

MEMORANDUM

All: Thank you all for your involvement in the Communications Training Session. Overall, the session was very effective on various levels. It was terrific to see so many contributing their stories, ideas, and opinions. It also was very beneficial to the group to present each question and gain ideas from Richard Zeoli, an experienced and well-known communications expert, and discuss how to deliver the message, consistently with thorough explanation.

As you are aware, this is very important to Genesis as a growing firm. It was critical to determine consistent responses and gain tips on how to deliver them successfully.

This session has increased our communication skills both internally and externally and enabled the directors to share their thoughts to their respective teams. If we practice our skills, do our "homework," and critique one another after each event or important meeting, look out … our vision can be realized within the year! Therefore, compiled below for your reference is a summary and the requested "action items" taken from the session. Looking forward to all of you becoming walking, talking, marketing machines!!!

Who is Genesis? What does Genesis do?

Response: Genesis is a multidisciplined professional services firm that handles engineering, surveying, and architecture.

- Back up this statement with three specific project examples. It is very common for people to hear things in groups of three.
- When speaking to larger clients, tailor the message to their needs: Genesis is a multidisciplined professional services firm, and its vast experience includes the Second Avenue Subway, Boston "T" extension, and the Baltimore Expressway. So, we have the capability to handle even the most complex projects.
- When speaking to smaller clients: Genesis is a multidisciplined professional services firm with a local presence. Our municipal experience includes Main Township Streetscape Design, Sunny Lane Bridge Design, and Soldiers Memorial Park Landscape Design. We have the capability to design projects that reflect the individual needs of the community.

What size company is Genesis?

Response: We are a growing firm, and this ensures that we will meet the goals, objectives, and needs of our clients.

- Our people are our strength. Relay our years of experience, accomplishment, and the success of team members.

- When speaking to larger firms, stress the recent new hires and new office openings.
- When speaking to smaller clients, remind them we are still small enough to provide the personalized service they have come to expect from Genesis.

What makes Genesis different from the other firms?

Response: Genesis delivers a hands-on team. We are the people who carry through the project from start to finish.

- All face-to-face contact is between the client and us. We do not pass the project on to someone else. We do not bait and switch.
- Introduce all key team players from the start. Always use the three key phrases to describe our work ethic:
  - **Hands-on** (example: Jim's role as project manager on the tunnel)
  - **Involved** every step of the way (example: Bob's role on the bridge project)
  - **Teamwork**—everyone is a partner. Due to our outstanding teamwork, Genesis has never failed to obtain an environmental permit on any project.

What are some of the stories of Genesis's success we would like to share?

- Provide three success stories that will appeal to a smaller potential client (municipal level or small firm).
- Provide three success stories that will appeal to a large potential client (major engineering firm we would like to partner with).

- How do we demonstrate our worth to larger firms of over ten thousand people?
- How do we sell ourselves to small towns of less than ten thousand people?

Response for large targets:

- Demonstrate how we can win!
- Pitch success we have had on large projects with large clients. Use words like "partner" and "team" rather than "assist" or "support" or "help."
- Do not make it seem Genesis is second tier.

Response for small targets:

- Local presence.
- Dedicated project manager, single point of contact.
- High level of client service.

We have completed the work successfully, gaining more work from the client because we completed the project on time and within budget.

What is Genesis's vision for the future?

Response: Genesis will grow from the preeminent regional engineering firm and gain a *nationwide presence.*

- As directors, bring vision to your team and believe in our success. Move from "dream" to "vision" to "state of mind." A dream happens subconsciously with your eyes closed. A vision is a tangible goal. Your audience will tend to follow those who give a "clear" vision.
- Where do you see Genesis in five years?
- What will others be saying about Genesis in five years?

Why are Genesis's people important to the process?

Response: Our people are our greatest strength.

- Genesis has developed a climate to attract and retain the best individuals and challenge them with the best projects.
- Some important points to remember:
  - Talk in terms of accomplishment and how the team has overcome challenges.
  - Define responses by showing strengths. The strength of our people is our advantage versus the larger competitors.
  - Stay on message and tailor the message to the right audience.
  - Know your audience before you walk into the room.
  - Be concise. Leave them wanting more.

★ ★ ★

The memorandum demonstrates that Genesis learned a great deal about how to tailor the message for the specific audience and how to stick to that message. They also learned how to communicate their vision externally and internally. It was a very successful training seminar, and I have since worked with several of the newest managers. The firm continues to grow to new heights as they land both small and large clients because their message is always tailored to highlight their relevant strengths depending on the target audience.

Visuals

Prior to the training, Genesis Engineering fell into the trap, like many organizations do, of focusing on listing experience and capabilities rather than telling stories that *prove* the company's experience and capabilities. Anyone can tell you he or she can do something. Someone can tell you he is capable of orbiting space, but when an astronaut tells you the story of what life was like on a shuttle that was actually orbiting the earth, who has more credibility?

So many organizations are caught in this trap, yet they wonder why their business isn't seeing the growth it is capable of achieving.

The answer lies in showing rather than telling. There is an old saying in acting: "Show, don't tell." Basically, this means that as an actor, you must show the audience how you feel, rather than telling them. One of my favorite scenes in movie history is so subtle that unless you are obsessed with the movie, you might miss it. Yet it is one of the reasons *The Godfather* is so successful.

In the scene, Michael Corleone, who is destined to become the ruthless leader of the Mafia, is still outside the family business and goes to the hospital to see his father, Vito Corleone, who has been gunned down by rival gangsters. Realizing that no one is guarding his father and that people are coming to kill him, Michael stands outside the hospital along with the family baker and pretends to have a weapon as the carload of gangsters arrives to carry out the deed.

Seeing the "armed" guards, the driver pulls away. Afterward, the baker is shaking so badly from nervousness that he cannot light his cigarette. He fumbles with the lighter and Michael takes the lighter and effortlessly lights the cigarette for him. Michael glances at his own hands to realize that they are not shaking.

Film students and scholars recognize that the scene shows that this was not a terrifying experience for Michael and actually foreshadows his inevitable turn toward violence. It is incredibly effective and one of the reasons that the movie won so many Academy Awards. Yet, it would not have been as effective if Michael had instead said, "Wow, that just didn't bother me in the least! In fact, I kind of liked it!" That is a perfect example of "show, don't tell."

Yet so many companies try to tell their experience and qualifications instead of actually showing their experience and qualifications. This often backfires in PowerPoint slides and handouts.

I've actually seen companies put things on a slideshow such as:

- Our company has the experience to build this project.
- We worked on three highway projects this past year.

And then they will put up a slide that shows a picture of the highway. Nice visual, but not at all effective. Even though it is a visual, it is an attempt to tell rather than show. Herein lies the rub of relying on visuals like PowerPoint and storyboards in a presentation.

I told Genesis that I don't particularly like the use of PowerPoint presentations, and the company management said it was absolutely critical for them when they are making a presentation. It might be, but it's no excuse to rely on PowerPoint or visuals to do the presentation *for* you.

Pictures may tell a thousand words, but let's go back to the astronaut analogy for a moment. We can see a picture of a man walking on the moon and it says one thing to us. But when we hear Neil Armstrong tell the story of walking on the moon, it becomes entirely more meaningful. This is the reason that his famous quote, "One small step for man, one giant leap for mankind," resonates so powerfully even to this day. It tells a story of tremendous accomplishment that a simple picture cannot tell by itself.

Please do not misunderstand me. Pictures have a place, but unless you are giving a presentation on the power of pictures, as a presenter you should not rely solely on them. That's because a story, along with a picture, does so much to prove your point and make the presentation that much more valuable than a picture alone.

A better way for the engineering company to tell its story would be to create a slide that says, "With more than forty years of experience, including multimillion-dollar projects, we have the expertise to do this job."

Perhaps Slide 2 could show the picture of a project that was once dilapidated, and then the speaker can tell the story that accompanies the visual of how challenging it was to face this project and iron out a plan for fixing the structure. Most presenters will simply show the slide and allow the audience to form its own opinions. Some audience members will be impressed, but others will not be. But when the speaker shows the visual, tells the story, makes it personal, and puts it into human terms to which we can all relate, that speaker is taking the visual to the next level.

I recently watched a PowerPoint presentation in which the speaker put up a slide of the game of "Pong" on the screen, then flashed to a slide of the game "Donkey Kong," then a slide of a modern-day game in which the character looked incredibly lifelike.

The caption above the Pong slide read, "first video game." On top of Donkey Kong, it said, "innovation advances," and on top of the modern slide it said, "quality enhancements."

The speaker went through each slide and then tried to tie the games into our health care system to attempt to prove his point, which was, "By using electronic records, we will get better health care."

If you were an audience member and were confused, you were not alone. Most of the people in the audience were confused, and the presentation was not effective. I have no doubt that someone very creative worked hard to insert those visuals, thinking they would be interesting. And while perhaps they were, they certainly did not do a good job of telling the story.

However, when the speaker used an actual testimonial from a person who had lost all her medical records in a natural disaster but was still able to continue to receive health care because her doctor had backed up her records electronically, a lightbulb suddenly went off in the room, and everyone understood the importance of using electronic records.

One story was much more effective than several pictures of a giant ape throwing barrels.

My advice to this presenter was simple: Get rid of the PowerPoint and instead create a live video testimonial of an actual person telling her story. Or, if cost is a problem, read her testimonial to everyone in the room. Do not make the mistake of relying on PowerPoint or visuals to tell a story. Even though they are visuals, they wind up telling rather than showing. That is the irony of relying on visuals. The presenter in this case tried to tell us that innovation took time by putting up a cute picture of Donkey Kong when in reality, the patient testimonial accomplished everything he was trying to prove in a fraction of the time.

As for the engineering firm we talked about earlier in this chapter, I would advise the presenter or presenters to certainly show the pretty picture of the highway the firm designed, but I would also encourage them to use it as backdrop and to have someone share the story of how the highway was designed. Share the challenges, the hurdles, the victories. These stories, as we learned in Principle 6, will do so much more to prove credibility and experience than a picture ever can.

Again, we love the picture of the astronauts walking on the moon, but we can't relate to it. We can, however, relate to the fear they experienced before taking off from earth. We can relate to the euphoria they felt when they took that one small step, and we can relate to the feeling that their mission had a purpose much larger than themselves.

The picture as a background is great. And combined with the story from the astronaut who was actually there or from the person in mission control who gave the prelaunch countdown, it is powerful and will ensure your audience is interested, engaged, and convinced of your credibility, ability, and experience.

PRINCIPLE **7**
ANTICIPATION

Always Leave Your Audience Wanting More

Be sincere. Be brief. Be seated.

—**Abraham Lincoln**

ANTICIPATION

One of the most valuable lessons I have learned in my years of communications is that when it comes to public speaking, less is usually more. Rarely, if ever, have I left a gathering and heard someone say, "I wish that speaker had gone on longer." However, I imagine that we've all probably heard many times, "Am I glad that speech is over. It seemed to go on forever."

Today, as speakers, we're competing for the attention of audience members who have BlackBerrys and phones that get e-mail and mobile Web and text messages. We've already discussed people's increasingly limited attention spans, and the longer the speech, the more opportunity for people's minds to wander. In most cases, the more a speech drags on, the less inclination listeners will have to try to stay focused. Most points can be made relatively briefly, and, oftentimes, long-winded speeches are due more to the speaker's desire to hear himself or herself talk than the need to convey information.

So, surprise your audience. Always make your presentation just a bit shorter than anticipated.

This may come as a shock, since most people feel they need a tremendous amount of time to get their point across, but if that is the case, then your speech is probably filled with cute stories or funny lines that serve no purpose in helping you prove your point and stay on message. We hold an audience's attention not with cute stories and funny jokes but with interesting, relevant points that prove the point of our thesis.

Besides, if you've followed the first six principles, then you already have your audience's attention and interest.

Remember, you've given up the notion of trying to be a great speaker and you have learned simply to be yourself and to have a conversation with your audience. You've practiced in the weeks and days leading up to the speech. You have visualized yourself in front of the audience giving an effective speech, so your mind is prepared for this crucial moment. You understand that if you make mistake or two, that's okay, because you understand that making mistakes is part of the process and part of what makes you a human being capable of relating to an audience full of other human beings.

You've become a storyteller who has learned how to make your speech personal. And you have found a way to relate your speech to your audience members and show how it benefits them. So by using the seven principles, you already have your audience members' interest. But even with their interest, it's better to leave your listeners wishing you had spoken for just a few minutes more than squirming in their seats waiting for your speech finally to end.

Please take a moment to think about what you believe most audience members are thinking during a speech. How about you as an audience member? Which is usually more important to you: the information conveyed or the length of time it takes to convey it?

People ask me all the time, "How long should a speech be?" My answer is this, "Long enough to convey all the necessary information and not a second longer." As speakers, we must always maintain the goal of getting in and getting out. And of course convey the information somewhere in between. Do it in a way that's informative. Make it enjoyable, and then give your listeners the opportunity to get on with their lives. If you can do this as a speaker, you will leave your audience wanting more, and you will leave them happy that they had the opportunity to listen to you speak. Perhaps most important, you will never hear anyone say, "Wow, that speaker loves the sound of his own voice!"

From Theory to Practice: Making It Work

The Speaker Challenge

If someone gives you twenty minutes to speak, ask how firm this time limit is. In some instances, the event coordinator will expect you to fill all twenty minutes, but in the majority of cases, you will be given a time range. An example is ten to fifteen minutes.

If you know the time range is flexible, that is your opportunity to speak to the audience for only ten minutes and leave everyone wishing you had spoken for the extra five.

That said, however, proper speaker etiquette requires pleasing your host. If he or she really expects you to fill twenty minutes of time, you should do your best to come close. But before you even agree to speak, you should negotiate this. Try to avoid putting yourself in a position in which you are trying to fill time. Instead, think about how long you really need to get your message across, and ask the organizer if it is okay if you speak for that length of time.

You might phrase your request as follows: "Thank you for inviting me to speak about my business, and I appreciate your offering me a full twenty minutes of time! I really need only about ten minutes to get my point across, though. Is that okay with you?"

In most cases, the event organizer will say yes, as this frees up time for the organization to conduct other business and for members to network or eat their lunch. If you are being paid to speak for an hour, however, you should fulfill the terms of your contract and speak for an hour. Most of us won't have to worry about this, however. Instead of orating for pay, we will be giving a presentation to the company, conducting a community mortgage seminar, speaking at a chamber of commerce dinner, or giving a toast at a wedding.

In all of those instances, adherence to Principle 7 will leave people wanting to hear you speak again.

So how do you know when enough is enough?

To begin, you have to make sure you have effectively proven your thesis—the central component of your message.

If you haven't proven your point, you need to rework your speech and see what's missing, but if the speech is already quite long, then you need to determine what can be cut. The litmus test is simple: Does this line prove my point and keep me on message? If the answer is yes, keep it. If the answer is no, cut it. Remember, put the "lighter" components of the speech in your opening, and reserve the meat and potatoes for the body of the speech.

This rule is simple, but unfortunately, most speakers will not adhere to it. Instead, they will be right in the middle of proving their point to the audience and then feel the need to go off on a tangent that has nothing to do with supporting their main thesis. For example, they might tell a story that, while possibly entertaining in and of itself, has nothing to do with the core message of their speech. Most speakers do this because they think it's the only way to keep the audience with them. Believe me, it's not. If you are giving your audience members relevant information, keeping the speech interesting, and staying on message, they will be with you. But if you go off on an unrelated tangent, insert a funny story about your vacation in a part of the speech that has absolutely nothing to do with anything you are talking about, or throw in a joke for no reason other than to try to make the audience laugh, then you will lose your listeners, because you are not respecting their time.

Once you are certain that you have proven the point of your thesis and when you have come to the end of the speech, then it is time to summarize your point and get out as quickly as possible. This is the place where the audience members will recognize the speech is coming to an end and prepare their minds for the conclusion. So give them what they want. Thank them for their attention, thank the event organizer, plug your business or Web site, and walk off the stage to a round of enthusiastic applause.

"One last point!"

Please don't ever be a speaker who uses the phrase, "One last point," or a variation of the line such as, "One last point and I'll finish up," or "I'm almost finished, but first I want to tell you about…"

When you let the audience members know the end is near, but don't then give them the end, you have done something truly unforgivable as a speaker. You have told your audience to expect one thing and then delivered another.

You have broken the attention-connection and allowed listeners to realize that the end is coming. In most cases, they will then say to themselves, "Okay, good, I'm ready to go."

"I'm ready to eat."

"What time is it?"

"Where is the bathroom?"

Rarely will they think, "He just said last point … I better tune in really closely now because this must be the best point."

Just the opposite. We somehow know that last point is the point we can brush over, because if it were so important, it wouldn't be the last point.

When you have the audience's attention, when you make that attention-connection, your job is to hold it and not to give your audience a glimpse of the closing curtain. Think of your favorite movie and ask yourself if it would have had the same effect on you if right before the climax of the movie, words came up on the screen that said "FINAL SCENE" or "ONE MORE TO GO AND YOU CAN GO BACK TO SHOPPING!"

Your speech is no different. Hold your audience's attention.

The Audience Hoped the Man from Hope Would Finish.

One of the greatest examples of this principle has to be the 1988 Democratic National Convention, when a young Bill Clinton gave the nominating speech for Michael Dukakis. Now, whether you like Clinton's politics or not, most people consider the former president to be a truly gifted speaker, and he partially attributes this to learning from a mistake he made. As *Time* magazine put it in 1992: "Clinton's speech droned on through thirty-three minutes that seemed about five times as long; the cheers that erupted when he said 'in conclusion' appeared to toll the knell of any hopes he might have had to succeed in national politics."

Trust me, you don't want anyone ever to refer to your speech as having droned on. And you don't want people to erupt into applause when you say, "In conclusion..."

Clinton learned the hard way the same lesson that many of his predecessors had known.

Consider that some of the greatest speeches of all time—those that have literally altered the course of history—were far shorter than the average speech you hear at a business luncheon.

For example, let's take a look at speeches from three of our nation's greatest presidents:

Abraham Lincoln—The Gettysburg Address is considered to be one of the single most important speeches in the history of the United States, yet it is only ten sentences and 272 words long. It took President Abraham Lincoln a little more than two minutes to deliver this speech that forever impacted the course of the Civil War.

Ronald Reagan—"Mr. Gorbachev: Tear Down This Wall." Did you know that President Ronald Reagan's speech, given on June 12, 1987, at the Brandenburg Gate in West Berlin, was only 2,703 words? Of these, the six words quoted above resonated loudest around the world and helped usher in the fall of communism.

George Washington—And here's a fun fact: the Father of our Country, President George Washington, gave an inaugural address that was only 135 words—the shortest on record.

The point is simple: It's not quantity but quality that matters. This is incredibly important for everyone to remember when standing up to sell a business, a product, or even a talent. So keep in mind this fundamental rule: A speech should be long enough to convey all the necessary points and not a second longer.

Follow this principle, and you will find it easier than you ever imagined to hold your audience's attention and be an effective communicator.

T HE MASTER COMMUNICATOR

A Parable of Principles in Action

THE MASTER
COMMUNICATOR

*T*he man in the third row started to doze off. He didn't plan on dozing, but the speaker he was listening to was going on for way too long. "The auditorium is so warm," he thought to himself, "and besides, I was up last night working on that project."

The speaker at the podium was beating this point about Sarbanes-Oxley to death. All John could hear was "regulation," "compliance," "accounting," "fees." It was enough to make him scream.

Why do I have to be here? Oh yeah, continuing education credits, I forgot.

John started imagining that the speaker had lost his voice. It was all he could to avoid running out of the room. He glanced at his colleagues. Are they tuned into this guy or are they faking it, too?

Oh man, how much more of this do I have to take?

On and on, and on, and on. There seemed no end in sight.

Forget it; there is no point trying to fight it. *The drowsiness was overtaking him now, the lids on his eyes growing heavy with each boring, monotonous syllable the speaker threw out.*

Within a few moments, John was asleep.

Dreaming now, of a time way back. Of a time he went on a journey that changed him forever. In many ways, it changed his life for the best, but in some ways, it caused him immeasurable strife, as he now couldn't tolerate speakers like this bozo anymore.

A distant time. Right after college.

Everything seemed bright about his future. After he graduated with honors in finance, the world was his to conquer. No fear. Well, one, but a common one. So common, in fact, that most people say it is more fearsome than death. But John didn't really fear it per se; he just didn't understand it. He didn't care, really. He had taken the mandatory public speaking course and earned his three credits. He'd learned all about how to write a great outline, and he'd heard how great it was to have the butterflies but to make sure they all flew in the right direction, whatever that meant.

He'd learned how to write and give a speech as his class assignment. About? What was it again? My summer vacation? No, wrong decade. I don't remember, but it had a great outline.

How was my delivery? Well, let's see, I had five minutes to speak, I know that. The instructor knocked me down a grade because I only spoke for three, that's right. He said that I didn't fulfill the assignment, but I thought brevity was the soul of wit. Oh well.

How did I feel up there that day when I gave that speech? I was scared, right? Me, the fraternity president, whom everybody loved. The natural salesman, yet I was scared. What was I supposed to do again to get over it? Be prepared, right. If I was prepared to speak, then I'd be fine.

That worked well in the classroom, but what if I don't have time to prepare? What if I have to stand up at a company meeting and give an overview of my department and I have no time to prepare? What if I see the CEO in an elevator and he asks me to give him my impressions of the company? Where on earth will my outline be then?

It was too much. I got a B in that class. Well really, when would I need public speaking anyway? It's not like I'm going to run for office or anything.

John shifted in his seat as the speaker droned on for another five minutes while dull slides shone on an enormous screen. The speech was illustrated almost to the point of being absurd.

I needed it, though, didn't I? That first job interview. I had no idea there would be four people in the room. I figured a job interview would be just one person. But there were four. Four top managers. And I realized as they were staring at me while I spoke that, even though I was sitting down, holy cow, I was giving a speech, wasn't I?

Butterflies, just fly north. Or is it south? I don't remember.

Where's my outline? I don't have an outline for this. I had no idea this was going to happen. I'm not prepared. How could anyone be prepared? I'm nervous. I'm speaking to this group, and they're staring at me. I can be great, just be great, John, you can do it.

I'm giving a speech, aren't I? I mean I'm on a couch and they are in chairs, but I'm giving a speech about myself and my background! Should I stand up? That would be formal, right? Too formal, but this feels weird. WHERE IS MY OUTLINE?

John sat up in his chair, startled and sweating. A few of his colleagues looked his way and gave him disapproving glares. He looked straight ahead.

The speaker was still going on. A few others had also nodded off. It was really hot in there.

Too hot. He was back in the late nineties. Leaving the office.

He didn't get the job.

How would he have, really, after that performance?

But it wasn't as bad as two summers ago at the company retreat, after he had made vice president of investment management and had to give a speech about his boss.

Why did I try that joke about his shore house?

Dumb, dumb, dumb. I thought he would think it was funny.

It was a beautiful day. The sun was shining down over Montauk that afternoon as the lighthouse stood in its protective pose to the east. How happy am I? Vice president at thirty-five. And I have the honor of introducing the senior VP to the rest of the company. Wow! This is terrific!

How did I get here? Doesn't matter, I'm here.

I made my outline, I know exactly what I am going to say. I wrote down all my points, and I'm prepared. I'm terrified, though. Those butterflies are all flying. Why am I still nervous if I have my outline? I'm prepared.

"Hey John, enjoying the End?" Walter Sullivan, the VP of Mergers and Acquisitions. Such great clothes, such poor choice in spouses. He was on his fourth now.

"Love it here, Walter. I only hope that one day I can own a place out here."

"Keep up the good work and I know one day you will," he says. "You are going places."

"Thank you, Walter."

"Look, John, I know you are introducing Mac today. Do you have a joke in mind? Something funny you are going to say?"

"Well, Sir, I …"

"It's just that we could all use a laugh. Think of something witty."

And with that he was gone. On his way to grab another Bellini at the outdoor bar.

A joke? I can do that. What can I say? It's not on my outline. What should I say? There's so many ways to make fun of this guy. I mean, he's all alone, his wife left him. All he has is his money. That's it. I'll say something about that. Okay, good. I can improvise.

Walter Sullivan took the podium and asked everyone to please gather round.

"I want to thank all of you for coming today. We've had an outstanding first and second quarter, and today is your day to enjoy each others' company, and my booze. In all seriousness, I want to introduce to you a young man from our investment banking division. John is a bright guy, he just made VP and we expect great things from him. Come on up, John."

The applause was tepid. The jealousy of his peers seethed through the crowd.

John walked up and shook Walter's hand. He pulled his outline out of his poplin sports coat and started to read it.

There was no podium.

There was no microphone.

Heck, they were on a beach.

There were those darn butterflies though. They were back.

"Thank you Mr. Sullivan. Today we are here to honor our Senior VP of Finance, Macarthur 'Mac' Collins. I have a lot of great things to say about Mr. Collins, and one of them is that we can all rest assured our money is safe in this company. I mean, his wife left him,

his kids left him, but his money has stuck around all these years, so that has to say something about his skills, right?"

There are moments in life that you can literally see the words you just spoke leave your mouth, slowly make their way across the time-space continuum, and enter the ear canals of the people in your direction. If there were a way to jump across the room and grab those words, like a child grabbing giant alphabet soup letters with his plastic spoon, John would have done it in a heartbeat.

The faces. The jaws. The jaws on the faces. Dropped.

Like his career prospects.

Walter Sullivan looked annoyed. Visibly annoyed.

The crowd just stared.

Did I say that? It didn't come out right. That was supposed to be funny. That was supposed to be a cute line.

What? Mac is staring at me. He doesn't look angry. Maybe he's okay. Maybe he got it. Maybe he's … welling up? With tears? No, not possible. The man is one of the Forbes Richest Men on the Planet. He's worth more money than everyone here combined. How could he be … ?

Was that a tear?

Did I make this man, this giant of a man, cry?

Just keep going.

"But seriously folks, Mac is a truly tremendous man. He built this company, and we all owe him a tremendous debt of gratitude. Please join me in welcoming Mr. Collins."

The applause was enthusiastic, and Mac Collins did his best to look happy as he took the microphone.

"Since John didn't get a chance, let me thank Walt for his hard work setting this party up for everyone. And I want to thank the

staff. They are working so hard to make this day a truly special day. John jokingly talked about my personal life, and it's true that this company has always been a priority for me, but I want you all to know something. Family comes first to me. And you are my family. And I am so happy to be here today. Thank you.

"And John, I want you to know something. You can joke about me, you can joke about my marriage, but never, ever, make a joke about my children. I lost them because …"

"John, hey man, wake up, you're snoring."

Roy Cassidy shoved his elbow into John and looked around the room. The speaker was still going.

"This is boring, I know, but you are getting looks."

"Sorry, Roy, but this is painful and this guy needs some serious help up there. Are you even getting anything out of this?"

"No, but we all need the CE credits, John. You know that."

"Right, okay. Wake me if I start to snore again."

The line at the coffee shop was long, but John didn't mind. They made the best cappuccino in the city, and it was still a lot cheaper than the national coffee shops, and for a guy out of work, or in between jobs, that meant a lot.

"Just in between jobs, that's all," he thought as he flipped the jobs section of the New York Times. *"Nothing to worry about."*

He barely noticed when the man sat across from him and put his double espresso down on the little two-person café table. John looked around the room. It was okay to share space if the place was packed, but it was two p.m. and nobody else was in here.

Maybe I'll ignore him and he'll go away.

"Any good leads in there?" the man asked.

John tried not to look directly at the man, but he glanced up just long enough to see that the man was wearing jeans and a blue blazer. Italian, probably Brioni.

"Not much, economy is slow. Market's been down."

"So you're in finance?"

"How did you know that?"

"You just told me. I listened to what you said."

"Right. Thanks."

"You know, you probably want to make sure you don't blow the next interview or make a joke to offend anyone."

"Excuse me?"

"I mean, I'm just offering some advice, but do what you want."

"Who are you? What are you talking about?" John asked as the anger began to show on his face.

"I'm a friend. Call me Smith. I'm here to help."

"Who sent you?"

"A very close friend asked me to drop in on you. You are an incredibly bright man, John, but you have a fundamental flaw that is going to keep catching up with you. Your communication skills need major help."

John shifted in his chair, making sure no one was secretly video-taping this. "So you're a coach or something?"

"Sort of. But a little more. I don't normally take on clients, but in this instance, I am making an exception. If you're ready to stop sabotaging yourself with your words, come by my office tomorrow at five p.m. Bring a notebook."

"What kind of notebook?" John asked skeptically.

"The kind you write in," said Smith as he threw his business card on the table and started to walk toward the door. "And, John, I

have no time or patience for skepticism. People who think they know everything already have no business trying to benefit from my training. Because they won't."

With that, Smith exited the coffee shop.

The business card was plain white with black type. It simply read "Allen Smith," with an address for an office a few blocks away. John thought this was the height of lunacy and figured there was simply no way he would be seeing Mr. Smith again.

How wrong he was.

John lay awake that night. He couldn't sleep, and he was hesitant to take a sleep aid again. He kept thinking about what Smith had said. Sabotaging my life with my words. I'm not sabotaging it. I just made a few mistakes here and there, that's all. Smith is a nut job. I'm not going. Period.

Okay, I'm only going to explain that I have not sabotaged my life with my words. I've made a few mistakes along the way, but I have not sabotaged it.

John arrived in front of Smith's office and walked up three flights of stairs. Smith was waiting for him, a pot of fresh coffee ready on the counter. "You decided to see what I could teach you?"

"Look, I only came to tell you one thing, I haven't ..."

"Everyone who doesn't understand the principles is sabotaging their lives with their words John. Everyone—not just you. Don't take it so personally."

"How did you know I was going to say that?"

"Everyone says that. People's automatic first reaction is to be defensive about that statement. But the fact is, if you haven't learned the principles, then you are sabotaging yourself, because you are not living up to your full potential. And that is inexcusable."

"Is this about my stupid joke?"

"No, it's about what's inside you. It's about your potential. It's about the fact that you know that you have tremendous talent inside you and you are looking for a way to express it. I'm offering you a path, John. A path to being able to stand before an audience of five or five thousand and command a room. A path to enable you to look every person you meet in the eye and communicate with them. Not just talk, but really communicate. I am offering you a path to becoming a master communicator."

John's initial reaction was to walk away, but something about Smith intrigued him. Plus, the coffee was excellent, and as far as he could tell, Smith was not billing him for his time.

"What do I have to do?"

"Commit yourself. Commit yourself to learning seven principles of speaking that are essential to your journey. The work is difficult. The process can be long. The results ... well, they speak for themselves. That much I can say with certainty."

Principle 1: Perception

"Are you ready to begin your training?" Smith asked as John stood in front of the podium in the training facility.

"Yes, and I've prepared a speech like you asked me to."

"Excellent," Smith replied. "Rip it up."

"Rip it up? Why? I spent hours on this thing. I put a lot of time into this speech," John said anxiously.

"I know. I read it. It's a very good speech," Smith replied.

"Then I would like to know why on earth you would have me tear it up?"

"Because it doesn't sound like you. Because it isn't you. So, tear it up. Please."

Reluctantly, John tore up the speech and threw it into the garbage.

"Come on," Smith began, "we're going for a walk."

They walked out of the state-of-the-art training facility and out into the wooded area behind the office. Smith told John to take a seat on a wooden bench that looked as if it had survived many cold Adirondack winters.

"I need you to become someone different than who you have been when you have spoken before," Smith stated to a very confused-looking John. "For so many years of your life, you have always tried to play the role of the eager job seeker, or the up-and-coming junior executive, or the successful marketing executive. Now I need you to become something else for me in order for our training to be successful. So, are you ready to begin?"

For the first time, and it wouldn't be the last time, John began to doubt Smith's sanity and the point of this "training." After all, John had taken a few public speaking classes in his life. He'd studied the craft in college, and he'd even taken a well-known seminar that his company paid for. In all of those courses, he'd learned vital techniques that had helped him throughout his career. Why now, after all this time, had he taken time off from work to travel five hours north to Lake Placid to go on a "journey" to become a master communicator?

It seemed to John that maybe the best thing he could do now was get back in his car and drive home. But curiosity got the better of him, and he asked the question that would soon change everything he ever believed about public speaking.

"What do I have to become for our training to be successful?"

"Not what," Smith started, "Who."

"Okay, let me rephrase," John said while growing impatient. "Who do I have to become in order for our training to be successful?"

Smith paused for a few moments as he stared over the great expanse of the High Peaks.

He turned toward John and gazed intently in his direction.

"Yourself."

Silence.

Smith continued.

"For so long now, every time you've opened your mouth in public you have put on an act and tried to sound like a master communicator. The first principle you must understand, that you must master, is that there is no such thing. For you to be effective, John, you need to stop trying to be anything other than who you already are."

With that, Smith retreated back to the confines of the facility, leaving John to ponder these words while a cool Adirondack breeze swept over his face.

Principle 2: Perfection

"Focus," Smith said.

For two hours John was stuck in a tiny room on the far end of Smith's office and left to do nothing but write. Two hours. John felt anxious and was truly irritated by this treatment.

Smith's orders were clear: "Write down the mistakes you most fear making when you communicate."

John paced up and down inside the room, reluctant to disclose this information, but even more reluctant to search within himself and find his faults.

But Smith was insistent. John could not leave the sanctity of that office until he had completed the task.

So John went to work. He wrote down his fears and when he finished, marched proudly back to Smith's office to share the fruits of his labor.

"What is the first fear on your list?" Smith asked.

"I'm afraid I will stumble on my words."

"Why does scare that you?" Smith asked.

"Because if I stumble on my words, people will think I am an idiot."

"What else?" Smith asked.

"People will laugh at me. I will lose my credibility."

"People will laugh at you?"

"Yes. I'm scared. I'm very scared to make a mistake. I've made mistakes and they've been devastating to me. They've cost me jobs and interviews, and I don't want to make these mistakes again."

Smith then instructed John to make a list of all the mistakes he had ever made when he communicated and left the room. Again, John was alone.

This time John wrote furiously. He wrote with a passion and intensity he didn't even realize he had. He was angry now—at himself, and at those who had ever judged him for his mistakes.

He made the list and stared down at the paper looking at all the mistakes he had ever made. Then, he jumped out of his chair with great enthusiasm.

"Smith, get in here. I'm finished," he shouted with delight.

Smith walked in, and John proudly handed him the paper, like a son showing his father his first A.

Smith stared at the paper for several minutes then glanced over at John. "This is very good work. I can tell you put a tremendous amount of thought and effort into this."

"Thank you. I worked very hard on it."

It was at that moment that Smith took out a butane lighter and set John's work on fire.

"Hey, what are you doing? I poured my heart out into that thing! Stop it!"

Smith stared at him rather intimidatingly as the paper continued to burn and ashes fell all over the floor. He wiped his hands together and stomped his foot on the last of the burning embers.

"Sit down," he instructed John. "The sooner you realize what I am about to tell you, the sooner you will be free of your burdens and able to achieve effectiveness once and for all."

"That was my work. I'm really angry right now, Smith."

"Enough. I wanted you to see your mistakes go up in flames. I wanted you to understand that the only person who cares about what was written on that paper was you."

"You better believe I care, because I'm the one who wrote …"

It was at that moment John began to realize the point of Smith's exercise.

"When you make a mistake, no one cares but you." Smith explained. Once you understand this, you will be one step farther on your path toward becoming a master communicator."

"No one cares?" John asked incredulously.

"No one but you. And soon, even you won't care anymore. And therein lies effectiveness."

Principle 3: Visualization

He felt foolish.

John was a man with a business degree who spent most of his life studying in private school, traveling the world, and attending prestigious events with some of the most important people in New

York society. It was the world of rational thought that ruled him. And so sitting there, in the dark, on his back, with Beethoven playing softly in the background, he could only laugh at the absurdity of this exercise.

That's when the lights shot on, their intensity blinding him.

"Get up," Smith roared. "I'm not going to let you waste my time. I have far better things to do than this, and you aren't paying me."

"What did I do?" John asked, but he knew the answer.

"It's what you didn't do, or won't do." Smith replied back.

"I'm trying to do the exercise, really I am. It just feels stupid to me, that's all."

"Then we are finished here," Smith said and walked out of the room.

John waited a few minutes, believing that this was just another one of Smith's points and that he would soon be back in the room.

Minutes passed. Then more minutes passed. Still, no Smith.

John walked out of the room and called Smith's name, but there was no answer. He walked down the hall and knocked on the door to Smith's office. No answer. John lightly turned the handle on the door and pushed it open ever so slowly. Smith was not in his office, but John could not help but look at the pictures on the wall. Dozens of them. Maybe more. Pictures of Smith with other people.

"So the guy has an ego wall," John said lightly under his breath.

He walked closer to the photographs. He recognized the faces in the pictures. How could he not? They were famous. Some had gold medals around their necks. Others held trophies. Some of the faces he had seen on the pages of Fortune *and* Money *magazines. Others were famous politicians. A few were celebrities. The rich, the powerful, the famous, and the champions were on Smith's wall, and he was standing with them as if he were their best friend.*

Below the pictures were handwritten notes, signed by many of the same people who smiled back at John from the photographs.

"Smith, I would not have this trophy without you. You are truly the best mentor I have ever had. Thank you for everything."

"I never knew I had this much potential. Or rather, I did know, deep inside me, but somehow over the years I forgot about it. Thank you for helping me unleash it once again."

"To the master communicator—Thank you for making me complete the visualization exercise. I wouldn't be here today without it, and I've learned so much. Thank you for removing my doubt."

John felt Smith's eyes on him and sensed his presence in the room.

"All champions share a common trait, John," Smith said from behind him. "They are willing to remove their doubt and believe in the power of their mind. Those who fail, fail because they do not believe in themselves, in their own power, and in the power of the mind to create reality. These pictures never leave this office and only my students are allowed to see them. It is my hope that you will also make this wall someday."

John felt foolish. Here were some of the greatest champions from all walks of life—the arts, politics, sports, and business—and there was Smith standing with them.

John felt foolish for not believing in the exercise. He started to apologize, but Smith stopped him.

"Don't berate yourself. They didn't believe at first, either. It's hard for our rational minds to understand the power of visualization, but once we do, we gain the power to unleash our true potential. Now, are you ready to try again?"

Principle 4: Discipline

"Fore!"

The man on the fairway ducked out of the way of the ball before it crashed down on his golf cart.

"Nice shot, Smith," John said sarcastically as Smith threw his club into the woods for the second time that morning.

John was convinced Smith was not a golfer—not by any stretch of the imagination—and he figured a man like Smith had no use for the game and probably felt it was a complete waste of time. Still, John had convinced him that a relaxing time on the lush green fairway at the Lake Placid Golf Club was the perfect way to spend a beautiful afternoon.

"This game is childish. I don't understand why you play," Smith grumbled.

"Come on, Smith, lighten up. We're getting fresh air, and look at the view of the mountains."

"We can have these views back at the office."

John lined up his ball on the ninth tee, sized up his driver, and hit a great shot that sent the ball careening down the fairway at least 160 yards, maybe more.

"Nice shot," said Smith with little fanfare.

"Thanks. Look, don't get upset, I'm out here several days a week when the weather is nice, and I've been playing for years. It's a hard game to learn. You really have to practice. We'll go to the driving range later."

"How often do you go to the driving range?"

"I don't know, three to four nights a week? It's a great way to release tension. I need to devote more time to practicing my short game, though."

"Are you a secret professional golfer?" Smith asked with a smirk.

"Professional? Smith, come on, you've seen me play eight other holes. I'm just barely surviving out here."

"I'm just curious why you spend so much time practicing if you don't have aspirations to be a professional."

"I like it, and it's fun. Besides, if you don't practice, you don't improve. I don't care how good you are."

"Let me ask you a question," Smith said as he took hold of John's driver and began his walk to the tee, *"how often do you practice the art of effective oral communication?"*

"Practice? Never. Why would I? I communicate every day."

"But how often do you spend time practicing before you have to give a speech?"

"I don't know, maybe right before I have to give the speech, I'll read through it once or twice."

"So let me understand. You will practice this silly little game that does nothing to advance your economic well-being, but when it comes to communication, which will directly enhance your career, you don't practice?"

"Well, I never looked at it that way."

"This amazes me. You have the ability to practice your speaking on a daily basis without ever having to incur greens fees and you don't do it, yet your business demands that you be at the top of your game when it comes to communication and you don't practice except maybe once or twice before you give a speech?"

"I see your point," John said slowly.

"I have news for you, John. You are missing a golden opportunity. You view speaking as something you do every day, so you think

there's no need to practice. I view speaking as something you do every day, so you absolutely need to practice.

John nodded pensively.

"And I have more news for you, John."

Smith lifted the club behind his back and swung an absolutely flawless shot that sent the ball flying straight down the fairway and landing on the green.

John was flabbergasted.

"I'm actually a pretty good golfer, and I don't really find this game to be that silly. But I believe I have now proven my point. Care to make the remaining nine holes a little more interesting?"

Principle 5: Description

"I wasn't always a master communicator," Smith said as the day's training ended and he and John started to walk back to the office.

"Oh no? I figured you were coaching people since you were born."

"I had a teacher, just like you have now. It was many years ago when my wife and I owned a small bed-and-breakfast not too far away from here. Before she passed on, business was good. We had our ups and downs, and we struggled at times, but overall, we found success. The times we shared together were very special before cancer got the best of her and she lost the battle. But she fought the good fight, and I will never forget her courage.

"It was some time after her passing that I decided to organize a charity event to raise money for cancer treatment, and I was invited to say a few words about the event at a local business organization. It was a golden opportunity to talk about the devastating effects her illness had on her life and what we could do to fight the disease. It

was important, John, and I didn't want to blow the opportunity. So I sought out a trainer.

"Together, we trained right here in these mountains, and he taught me a very special secret, which I will now share with you."

"Smith, I am so sorry about your wife. I had no idea."

"Thank you. I miss her. To honor her life and to encourage others to join the fight, I could have gone any number of ways in my presentation. I could have shown a lot of statistics or talked about her pain. I could have been very matter-of-fact about it all. And I suggested all of these ways to my trainer. But instead, he showed me a better route. He showed me how to tell a story.

"So, I told a story.

"I told her story. The story of her life. The story of a wonderful mother who loved her children with patience and grace. The story of a wife who was my best friend and stood by me every day. The story of my best friend.

"I told that story and ended with a plea for others to donate to this powerful cause so that other loving wives and mothers might one day not have to feel the pain she felt. Just as I have now told you a story about how and why I came to this place, I told her story.

"There was no greater way to honor her memory than with that story, and there was no greater way for me to teach you today the power that stories hold for us than by sharing this story with you. Ever since the first cavemen began to communicate, we have used the power of stories to convey ideas. The earliest paintings on cave walls were stories, and they reveal so much about the past. I wanted to leave the same lasting legacy, and I knew my wife's memory would always live on if I shared her story.

"You must share your story, too, John. A master communicator knows this power. Senses it. The audience knows too."

"When do I use this technique?"

"It is not technique, John. Techniques are for children. This is power. True power. The power of storytelling. You must use it to connect with your fellow human beings so that what you care most about will always live on.

"Our stories must always live on."

Smith began to choke up—the first time he had truly shown emotion to John. He walked toward the office, alone with his thoughts as the sun began its descent over Mirror Lake.

Principle 6: Inspiration

"So tell me why," Smith said, "Why is it that you want to learn to speak?

John started to explain to Smith how he wanted to use speaking to improve his life, to make more money, and to find a job worthy of his skills. He told Smith that he had watched very talented communicators rise through the ranks while his personal communication shortcomings seemed to hurt him. He wanted to change that. "I know I can do better. I know that I have it inside me to be a better communicator, to reach people, and to truly connect with them. I know that I should be able to reap the same rewards as the people who speak so well."

"John, you have come very far and learned a great deal in our training," Smith replied. "And you are so close to the finish line. I want you to understand I am truly proud of you. You now have five very powerful principles to use, to understand, to master as best you can. But you are missing a very crucial piece here, and until you understand the consequences of your actions, you will never be a truly effective communicator."

John waited patiently for Smith to continue. John had realized weeks ago that while Smith's approach was a tad unorthodox, his concepts were always accurate. John had learned that Smith truly understood how to connect to other human beings in a straight-forward and honest manner. Smith never used communication for manipulation, and he never tried to spin the truth. He didn't have to. He was arguably the most effective communicator John had ever met. Smith's command of the language and his ability to put words together for John's benefit amazed him.

When Smith offered advice, John felt as if the advice were tai-lored only for John. It was as if everything Smith spoke were only for John's ears. Did it make John feel special? Yes, in a way, but more importantly, it made John appreciate what Smith was saying. Other speakers would always cause John's mind to wander aim-lessly because he never felt connected to the message, but when Smith spoke, John felt a stake in what he was saying.

He didn't quite understand it, but he did know that his master had his best interests in mind, and that is what mattered most to John.

"I return to my earlier question, John," Smith began. "Why do you want to speak? Stand up and tell me about it, please."

By now, the ten-foot walk over the gravel path to a handcrafted wooden podium situated in front of the High Peaks was a piece of cake. The first couple of times John had made the walk, he had practically tripped on a large rock and jumped like a six-year-old when he startled a lazy black bear who was sunning himself on the rock.

"I want to speak to improve my life," John said. "I now under-stand the power of communication, and it is a power that I have inside me. Today, I am unleashing that power. I want to speak so I can achieve the same success, the same greatness, and the same fulfill-ment as the others who have learned to be master communicators. I

will speak to advance my position in the company. I will communicate confidently. I—"

"Enough! I've had enough!" Smith interrupted. "Who cares what you want out of it? Not me and not the rocks. I don't think your friend the bear cares much, either. Look at the mountains. Do they care? No! They do not care. And neither do I, and neither does the audience. It's not all about you. What is this, The John Show? *I don't remember ordering a subscription!"*

Normally John would have felt a tad humiliated at such a chiding, but since the rocks, bears, and mountains were the only ones who heard Smith's words, he chose to bottle his emotions and realize that Smith was right. For all of his life John had always made it about himself. He had always been inwardly focused. And this is what had gotten him into so much trouble on so many occasions. The reality, though, is that John thought that he was supposed to make it all about him. After all, he was the one up there speaking. He was the one getting all the attention. He was the one everyone would be looking to for words.

"Sit down, John," a calmer Smith said, "You have come so far, and your skills have improved, but you must resist the temptation to believe you are the most important person in the room simply because you are the one standing in the front of the room. You must understand this principle. You must engrave it into your daily living. You are not the most important person in the room. Not even close."

"Who, then, is the most important person in the room?"

"The audience."

Principle 7: Anticipation

By now, John was beginning to understand the challenges he continued to face as a speaker. There was no doubt in his mind that he possessed the ability to become a truly effective communicator. But there was still one crucial step in his training that he needed to take. Still one more leg on this all-important journey that would forever change the way he communicated. For this part of the journey, Smith handed him a gift. A very special gift, indeed.

"What is this?" John asked

"A gift."

"Yes, but what is it for?

"For your considerable progress and accomplishments."

"Smith, you shouldn't have. Who would have ever known you were that kind of a guy?"

"Open it."

John opened the plain white box and discovered a simple gold pocket watch, classic in its design and clearly weathered over time. Yet, it still shone beautifully in the midday sun.

"Wow. This is a beautiful watch. Thank you."

"You are welcome. But this is not just any watch. It belonged to my great grandfather. He passed it down to my grandfather, who passed it down to my father. And since I do not have a son of my own, I now pass it on to you for your care. One day, when you no longer need it, you too will pass it along. This is a special watch, and it should go with you on your journey toward becoming a master communicator."

John cradled the watch in his hand, absorbing the magnitude of the heirloom. It was beautiful, indeed.

"Smith, I truly appreciate this gift. I will carry it with me always."

John opened the watch and realized that it had been crafted so, when opened, it could stand upright on its own on a flat surface.

"This watch should be with you at all times," Smith said, "and it should be used every time you speak. Open it as you have now, and place it on the podium in front of you. Time is the last element you must master, and it is a most critical element. When used properly, time is your ally, ensuring you are connecting with your audience. When ignored or taken for granted, time becomes your enemy, and each minute you speak longer than you have to pushes you farther and farther away from the hearts of your audience. The connection you make with your audience is directly related to time. This is more than a gift, John. It is a tool. One of the most important tools you have in your public speaking arsenal."

John understood. He thought back to all the times he had simply lost track of time during a speech and spoken for too long. He thought of all the times he had had to sit through a speech, enduring a speaker who seemed to have no regard for his listeners' time and went on for far too long.

"When you speak too long, you do not respect the audience's time." Smith said. "And the moment you cross the time line, you lose your listeners. Keeping proper time is a delicate balance, and as speakers, we must always strive to maintain that balance."

"How do I reach that balance? What is the rule?"

"The rule is simple: always speak for as long as it takes you to convey your message, and not a second more."

With that, Smith reached over to the watch, closed it—sealing its face behind the golden door—and walked away.

John understood.

The True Journey Begins

"John, wake up, the speech is over."

"Finally. Wow, how long was I out?"

"A good thirty minutes. Trust me, I kept my eye on the clock because that guy went on forever. So I guess you got a lot out of it, huh?"

John wiped the cobwebs from his eyes, gathered his belongings, and started to walk out of the auditorium. "Going on this incredible journey with Smith, learning so much, and experiencing so much personal growth and transformation has made it so much harder to listen to ordinary speakers now," he thought.

Having learned the seven principles and absorbed their true meaning, John had become a truly effective communicator. There was no grand ceremony, no elaborate graduation event, no award. And in truth, he would never be called a master communicator. But the intangible awards were even better.

John learned early on during the seven principles training that there is no such thing as a master communicator. We can only master ourselves, but we can never master communication. We will make mistakes, as we are only human. But the irony, John now understood, is that making mistakes is what makes us truly effective communicators to begin with. But a master? Never. There is only effective. There is only being an effective oral communicator.

And John was. He had started a journey, but he knew that the journey would never be complete. He understood that he would have to practice—several times a week. He realized that he would spend great amounts of time before a speech visualizing his success and that he would achieve that success. He understood now, for the first time, how to connect with an audience. And he discovered a rich secret when he learned that at the end of the day, the speech was never about him; it was always about the audience. His role was merely one of service.

John walked the few short blocks back to his building and went straight into his office. The importance of this evening's event would not be missed. Tonight, he would give a speech on the financial state of New York City, and in the audience, among other key notables, would be the mayor himself. Was he nervous? Nah, why would he be? After all, he had visualized this opportunity years ago in his training with Smith. And he visualized it just this morning as he was preparing for this day.

He changed into his tuxedo, and as he was fastening the buttons, he repeated his personal affirmation statement, reminding himself that he was about to have a simple conversation with the audience. Grabbing his keys, he walked out of the office building and hailed a taxi for the short ride down to Cipriani.

Cipriani was packed that night with a virtual Who's Who of New York City's elite. Probably about six hundred people there by his count. A large audience. His largest to date. John began to feel nervous, but he passed up the complimentary champagne in favor of club soda and chose once again to repeat his personal affirmation. He looked around the vast expanse of this elaborate room that had once been home to one of New York's largest banks. The old teller windows still stood as a reminder of the building's former life. The imposing marble columns and high ceilings would normally be intimidating, but John had been here twice before. The first time was a month ago when he was offered the opportunity to speak, and the second was early this morning at about two a.m. when the custodial staff was cleaning up from a Guardian Angels Gala Dinner.

Both times he was here, he spent time learning every detail of the room to help his visualization exercise become reality. And both times he was here, he practiced his speech. The first night to the one lone custodian who was happy to accept the twenty bucks for keeping the place open a few more minutes, and last night to the entire custodial staff, who wanted to hear what their colleague described as a "great speech by a really nice guy."

The flashing lights of an NYPD car pulled up in front of the building, and a large black SUV right behind it indicated the arrival of New York's most important person. As His Honor the Mayor walked in, with his security team in tow, the lights began to flicker, indicating it was time for everyone to take their seats. It was game time. And John was ready.

He took his seat and began focusing on his Crucial 5s. It was game time, and he was a champion. The MC began to read John's biography. John felt a hand reach out to take his. "I look forward to your remarks," said the mayor. John thanked him and took a moment in his mind's eye to see himself talking to everyone, just like he had visualized on so many occasions.

"I am a champion, and I am ready. I have practiced this speech, and I am ready. There is nothing to be nervous about because I am just going to have a relaxed conversation with this audience. The size of the crowd doesn't matter. I am prepared. I am focused. I am an effective communicator."

"I am ready."

As the announcer introduced him, John walked to the front of the room, placed his gold pocket watch on the podium, looked out at the six hundred faces staring at him, and smiled.

He was ready.

CONCLUSION: COMPENSATION

The Reward That's Better Than Money

" *You give but little when you give of your possessions. It is when you give of yourself that you truly give.* **"**

—Kahlil Gibran

Conclusion:
Compensation

W hile putting these principles into practice will help you overcome fears and become a truly effective public speaker, let me encourage you to aim for an even higher purpose. As you work toward achieving your public speaking goals, consider using your gifts to help others. For example, I regularly volunteer my time training nonprofit leaders in public speaking. Usually, these leaders are responsible for vital fund-raising, and they need to be able to sell the message and mission of their organizations. The success of their fund-raising and, consequently, of their group's mission and vision is largely dependent on their ability to communicate effectively and persuasively.

A wonderful place for you to begin practicing may be volunteering to speak on behalf of the good works of a local charity, religious group, or civic organization. Many times, these groups could use a qualified speaker, but may not have the immediate resources to hire one. What better way to gain practice while supporting a good cause? It will be a tremendous way for you to practice your public speaking while using your gifts to help others.

Diane is one of my favorite pro-bono clients. She runs Pass It Along (PIA), a wonderful group whose mission is to provide a way for individuals to make a difference in their community through meaningful volunteer service. Founded in 2001, PIA serves three populations—volunteers, nonprofit community-based organizations, and individuals that are in need of volunteer support—and offers well-managed, meaningful, and flexibly scheduled service projects in ten fields of interest. Diane's spirit is absolutely contagious. She fills every room she enters with positive energy and truly inspires everyone around her—especially me!

I have the honor of serving on PIA's Advisory Board, and I also act as Diane's media consultant before she has to give interviews. It is often difficult for nonprofit organizations to afford public relations firms, and yet nonprofits almost always have a wonderful message of hope and inspiration to share. Talk about living up to Principle 6! The stories that Diane can share about how far her clients have come and the struggles and obstacles they have overcome are truly inspiring.

Recently, Diane flew to Colorado to participate in the national Hands On Network's annual conference. In addition to attending the conference, Diane was scheduled to give an interview on a national radio station regarding the good works of PIA. Before she left, I volunteered to play the role of the host, and I spent the morning before her trip asking her the kinds of questions I felt she would get on the show. Just having the ability to practice helped her tremendously.

In finding your own service niche, ask yourself if there is a local organization in your community that could benefit from your abilities. While many of these groups need donations, they also need time and skills. There are people who can benefit from your expertise, and I hope you will share your talents with them. Our journey toward being truly effective communicators will only be enriched by using our skills and gifts to improve the lives of others.

Just a few weeks ago, PIA hosted a national day of service, and I was asked to give a speech to a group of high school and college students on the power of making a difference in their community. I was honored to be part of the day and excited about the opportunity to help inspire these young leaders. You won't have to look very far to find worthwhile organizations that would benefit from your communications skills. Perhaps you can volunteer to speak on their behalf about their upcoming fund drive. Maybe you can volunteer to teach underprivileged individuals communication skills. Or you can follow the lead of a good friend I know who works with job applicants returning to the workforce after a divorce, job loss, or illness, and helps them prepare for interviews.

Now that you are well on your way to being a truly effective communicator, I encourage you to take the principles you have learned and share your communication gifts within your community. As an added bonus, it provides you with a tremendous opportunity to practice your skills and refine your message.

All we have to do is open our hearts and we will find opportunities that will help us grow not only as speakers but also as human beings.